#I'mUpset

#I'mUpset

TONI SERRANO

Copyright © 2019 by Toni Serrano

All rights reserved. No part of this book may be used or reproduced in any manner without written permission from the copyright owner.

First paperback edition November 2019

ISBN-13: 978-0-578-59382-1

This book is dedicated to everyone seeking the life they deserve to live.

Even if you don't know what that looks like right now.

Whether you think you deserve it or not, you do.

You are worth it. You can do this.

In Love & Truth,

Toni

When you don't go within,

you go without.

—Yogi Bhajan

TABLE OF CONTENTS

Preface i
Intro 1

PART I
Rediscover Your Native Self

Chapter One: On 9
Chapter Two: Mantras 25

PART II
Establish Trust: Align Mind & Body

Chapter Three: Spiritual Entrepreneur 61
Chapter Four: Get Stimulated 71

PART III
Identify & Change The Pattern

Chapter Five: Insecurities 83
Chapter Six: The Lies We Tell Ourselves 99
Chapter Seven: And I Never Told You 115
Chapter Eight: Gateway To Self 131

Chapter Nine: Toni-isms 139
#ShoutOuts 175
References 177
Appendix 185

Prologue

I was born in 1997. According to Google, I am technically classified as *Generation Z* rather than *Millennial*. But when do you ever expect us—*kids*—to ever follow rules or cite from credible sources? Plus, *Thoughts of a Gen Z* doesn't sound as nice.

    I suppose I did grow up with technology in my hands, though not as sophisticated in the current year of 2019. I remember playing Sega Genesis, PlayStation, and Game Cube (whoever had a GameCube was onto some next-level *stuff*) In third grade, my earliest, distinct memory of using a computer[1] is of a nearly transparent box, turquoise accents, a bitten apple on top, with a disk slot below the screen. I spent days in summer watching VHS—soon to be DVD movies.

    I got my first phone at 8 years old—a flip phone mind you. Relatively early, but necessary because my parents dropped me off at the wrong softball park an hour before my game started. You can imagine my emotions.

---

[1] iMac G3 in Bondi Blue.

I created my first MySpace around sixth grade. Of course, you know it was color-themed, with the newest song playing when you clicked on my profile.

I'd watch mostly music videos on YouTube—not so much has changed in that respect. I'd also watch anything on Nickelodeon, Disney, and Cartoon Network including but not limited to: *Spongebob, Avatar the Last Airbender, Wizards of Waverly Place, Cat Dog, Edd Ed and Eddy, Rocket Power,* and *The Power Puff Girls*. These shows later became *VH1 Top 100 Countdown, MTV Cribs, Rob & Big* and *Next*, to name a few.

But this is not what this book is about. It's really about how our generation is treated. No one respects us. Okay, so that's how we feel but most adults don't respect us. Many adults don't trust us. They don't believe in us. I mean really believe *believe*. They only believe in realistic dreams. Dreams that they see attainable in their eyes. And *#I'mUpset*, I mean, I'm more disappointed.

It's no secret that in the modern era, our generation is faced with massive trouble when choosing a career. Of the 66% of kids who even attend college after high school, only 33% of them actually graduate college. Of those graduates, 1 in 5 use their degrees. *I wonder what percentage of the 1 who use their degrees are happy.*

It's no secret that in the modern era, our generation is faced with massive trouble making our childhood dreams our reality. I'm lost, you're lost, we are all lost. All we want is to be happy—can you blame us? All we want to do is enjoy life and follow our dreams.

Prologue

You know, the dreams portrayed in all of our childhood movies and TV shows? The ones that say, "you can do anything, just believe!" That's why we have commitment issues. That's why we are indecisive. We're utterly afraid to stick to one thing for the rest of our lives. *Why?* Because we see, feel and hear all the regret, anguish and hate, that consumes the adults in our lives. Of course, we want to run as far as we can in the opposite direction. I ran blindly. I ran in the direction of what I thought to be my dreams.

There will come a day when you must choose the life you're going to live. This will be a very special day. It may come in the dead of night when you're lying there in silence—alone with your thoughts. It may come out of necessity. It may come when you least expect it. When it does come you may or may not be prepared. I know I wasn't.

I resisted it. I knew it went against everything I'd spent my entire life doing. I was terribly conditioned. I was so insecure and I didn't know who I was.

I was afraid. I tried to push it back. To no avail, it kept coming back. It kept pushing out.

I felt like we were literally thrown into adulthood, with no preparation, sink or swim. I swam, the wrong way. If the right side of the pool was happiness, I swam left. *Why?* I didn't know I could swim right.

The good news is, the choice you made that day, isn't set in stone, even if you believe it is. *Why?* Because there's this thing called a sledgehammer. There an even bigger thing called a wrecking ball. And no, I'm not referring to Miley Cyrus' song.

The good news is, you can change your choice—as often, as quickly, as many times as you want to. Which is why this book came to be.

One day I decided, "who cares, why not. I didn't want to be conditioned, I didn't want to be insecure, I wanted to be courageous, I wanted to be free, I wanted to be me." This book is how I got out. I am me, are you, you? *insert Rush Hour 3 movie scene*

I decided to dedicate my life to learning how to be happy. I spent years addressing these thoughts, learning from them, keeping what worked and letting go of what didn't. Initially, all these questions caused distress and unease, but in the end, I was happy.

I was going to live happy, whatever that entailed. But first I had to realize all the things that were making me unhappy—upset as the title states.

Initially, this book was intended to express all my thoughts and complaints about the modern-day era. But rather than create an entire book about suffering, I felt my efforts were better used to offer solutions.

I soon realized before I can help anybody else in this modern world, I must first help myself. In the words of Mahatma Gandhi, "[I] must be the change [I] wish to see in the world." The change I wish to see is a remedy to sadness, fear, pain, and suffering. So, I decided before I could answer any questions for others, I must first answer them for myself.

Thus, I trekked on an inward journey—silent to those who knew me—to rediscover my *Native Self*. A Self stripped from every societal convention. A Self raw and uncorrupted. A Self concerned with curiosity rather than condemnation.

Throughout my journey inward, I discovered happiness, love, and truth to be the solution to suffering. I also discovered that sustained happiness derives from leading a life of love and leading a life of truth. And after years of constant reflection, diverse education and obsessive record-keeping, I'm ready to share the findings with you. Here lie the remnants of my journey to me, scattered but still somehow mirrors everything that is me.

> *"We Have Two Lives.*
> *The Second Begins When We Realize*
> *We Only Have One."*
> *—Confucius*

INTRODUCTION

In order to be happy, you must simply—be yourself. When things are simple, it doesn't mean they are easy. I had no idea how to be me—as simple as it sounds. I was so afraid to be me. *Why?* Because I had believed all of our modern societal constructs. I believed that if I didn't go to college, somehow I was a failure. I believed that I needed to make tons of money in order to be accepted—in order to be respected. I believed that I had to sacrifice my happiness in the process. Do you see the trend? Do you see the pattern? I believed in the dreams of others. I needed to start believing in the dreams of *me*.

It's not straightforward in the modern era. It's simultaneously the easiest and hardest time in history to be *You*. It's the hardest because we are constantly bombarded with distractions. Distractions screaming for our attention and taking the focus off of ourselves. There are so many people in the public eye that we can aspire to be. There are so many things that we can aspire to do. It leads to overwhelm. Overwhelm breeds inaction. It's *#FirstWorldProblems* because we have so many possibilities, we can't decide.

It's the easiest time in history to be You because once you realize who you are, the tools available to foster your growth are bountiful. There is easy, fast and free access to everything you need to self-educate and flourish.

However, in the modern era, we are often misinformed and believe with blind faith. It's not your fault. We were doing what we *thought* we *should* be. No one ever taught us *how* to be happy. No one ever showed us the way.

I devoted myself to find a way—despite the modern climate. I learned that in order to be happy in this modern era, you must lead with your conscious heart. *Your what?* Your conscious heart. This requires coordination. It requires mindfulness, trust and change. All the while you must live in Truth and live with Love.

We've spent our entire lives leading with a brain that was taught how to think. We are spiritual beings living in a world that is not. Logic is relative, but Truth is definitive. We have been taught to live logically, but what happiness requires is Truth.

Happiness is a spiritual state of being. Our heart is associated with our spirit. Happiness does require work, but work from our hearts, not our brains. Unfortunately, our hearts are severely underdeveloped and uncoordinated.

In the past when we act from our hearts, often the outcome was unpredictable. *#I'mUpset* offers a solution: you can lead with your conscious heart and create a favorable, predictable outcome—happiness.

Introduction

If you want to be happy you must find out what makes you unhappy. Then, you must find out what makes you happy. You must find out what you want. To find out what you want—*what you really want*—you must master yourself. You must be able to become aware of all the influences you have in your life. You must dedicate your energy to learn any tools necessary to contribute to your growth.

When you master yourself you will be in control. You will bring what you want into your life. You will enjoy life.

If you want to self-help, you must be able to find help. You must be able to cultivate and nurture it. There are things you can pay others to do for you. The truth is, you can't pay anybody to cultivate your happiness for you. You must create it within.

You must go to school and master yourself. You must become the student of yourself. Study yourself. You must earn a Ph.D. in *You*. You must notice your patterns. You must make them more efficient and more conducive to your goals.

Well, what are your goals? In order to find them, you must first question everything. To find out which is truly you. What has been projected onto you? You must discern your true self from the projected fears, opinions and judgments of others.

But first, we must overcome our brain. Our brain intends to protect us and keep us alive. When our heart was in control we may have suffered heartbreak. Therefore, the brain does not trust our heart to lead.

First, we must rediscover our *Native Self*. A Self absent of societal conditioning, opinions, thoughts and beliefs of others.

Next, we must establish trust—so that the mind and body can align. The easiest way to align your mind and body is to embrace and grow into the person you truly are.

The last hurdle to overcome is that which makes us unhappy. The third section reveals the hidden sources of our unhappiness. Once we relinquish the behaviors, patterns and beliefs that make us unhappy, we can truly live in the present moment of happiness.

When we become coordinated and aligned, we can experience *intentional, sustained happiness*. We begin to experience the powerful effects of unconditional Love. We begin to experience the liberating power of Truth.

When we lead with our conscious heart, happiness becomes more than fleeting moments. Happiness becomes a sustained state of being.

So before we begin, take a moment to brainstorm a few reasons why you considered taking this journey. When you identify a strong purpose—a reason why you're doing something—you eliminate confusion. Remember simplicity is the key to happiness.

Perhaps you're reading this book because you wish to become a role model for your children. How can we tell our children to be happy if we are not happy within ourselves?

Perhaps you're reading this book because you wish to be happy for your partner. So that you two may enjoy your life together.

But if you're like me, I sought these tools for my *future* Self. *I was suffering*. There wasn't anything in the *present* moment I wanted to do anything for. Immersed in suffering, a part inside of me imagined there would come a day when I could smile again. I imagined a happy and free me. So I trekked on my inward journey for my *future* Self. For the day when I wasn't immersed in pain, I'd know how to be happy.

Find your why. Make it clear, make it concise. It helps to display your *why* in a place you'll see daily. I tattooed it on my body—of course, you don't have to go to those extremes.

Right now, make a list of all the things that make you happy. Make a list of all the things that make you unhappy. You will use this list throughout this book.

PART I

Rediscover Your Native Self

CHAPTER 1

ON

"One thing I know, that I know nothing."
—*Socrates*

How can we build awareness of the Self? Question everything! I've included the main topics I obsessed over in the past few years. These topics are where I found a lot of confliction[2].

The conflict between what my beliefs were and what my actions showed. Remember, we must establish alignment with the mind and body. Confusion interferes with this alignment. We must become clear on what the Self believes. Then, we can align our actions accordingly. When you develop the Self you're able to address attachments you were unaware of.

---

[2] Yes, I made up this word. Some have used it before, but my definition is different. My conflicts caused afflictions, so I combined them together. I will use this word throughout.

Sometimes, when people do or say things, we don't clearly understand them. For instance, life clichés. They don't explain it well enough, and we don't ask further questions. *Why?* Because we both don't know. One doesn't know how to explain it better and the other doesn't know how to ask. I sought to go into further detail about such topics.

Whether you initially believe this perspective or not. I encourage you to *consider* the perspective I present. In my family, when met with a debatable idea, we say *quizás*. Which translates to *perhaps*. Is there a *possibility* of truth?

The point of this chapter is to rediscover the Native Self. I've included a few brief topics which serve to stimulate you to go within yourself for the answers. The Native Self is devoid of any cultural or societal beliefs that have been projected upon you. Take what serves you and leave the rest.

~

ON HUMAN 2.0

Maybe we were savages at some point but now we have evolved. When our basic needs are met, I believe we all naturally want to love and give. It is the natural instinct of humans today to care for one another. It is a new trait of the modern-day human. Human 2.0, if you will. The update has occurred and you must delete the old data. It doesn't mean you must forget it, but it no longer serves you. The new data does.

It's 2019, there aren't any excuses for us to be rude, inconsiderate, greedy, judgmental, arrogant, naive or negligent to each other. I heard the excuse thrown out, "I don't have time." To this I thoughtfully dismiss. It's time to be held accountable. We must take action to be better, be mindful and be respectful.

People may think they're too busy to be courteous and happy. I wish they knew they weren't. We have everything at our fingertips. Are you too busy to grab food? No problem, order delivery. Are you too busy to go to the store? No problem, order online. Are you too busy to walk your dog or watch your kid? No problem, there's an app for that. These modern conveniences free up loads of time for us. Yet the number one excuse I hear is, "I don't have time." What is it that we are doing with our time? Is it really because we're all too busy to be a kind human? Does it really take that much effort? The truth is, it doesn't. If there's one thing we have plenty of, it's time.

We are in an era of unlimited *abundance* with the *scarcity* mindset more prevalent than ever. We have the most resources in history to embrace the *Human 2.0* within us. Prior to the internet, we would have to read huge books on topics we needed to know about. Now we simply watch a 5-minute tutorial on YouTube.

We can easily watch a 5-minute video on guided meditation and breathing. We could even watch a 5-minute video on healthy foods that increase our energy and mood. Better yet, we could watch a 5-minute video on how to address our emotions of stress, fear, anger and anxiety. A video that teaches us how to stop projecting our negativity onto others. But, sadly, we'd rather watch a viral video that ironically has over a billion views.

Perhaps we are naive that we are even being inconsiderate and rude to others. I'm tired of the excuse, "It's just human nature." If we know that humans are capable of being competitive and cold, can't we choose to be the opposite? Our primal instincts are rarely useful in the modern world. Can't we evolve from hunters and gathers to conscious, courteous, respectful beings? Do not be naive. Do not be negligent. We must Evolve—for evolution is our True *human nature*.

We are amid an era where we can experience massive evolution or massive complacency. We can hit two birds with one stone. Driving, for instance, what seems to be the most time-consuming task aside from sleeping. Simply listen to podcasts or audiobooks while driving. Perhaps they teach us to center ourselves. Or reflect on our thoughts. They may offer tools for achieving the life we most desire. Traits such as consciousness, respect and care have always been attainable. The problem is, we'd rather be naive than accountable.

While there are *new* traits of *Human 2.0*, there are also old traits that haven't disappeared. If anything, these traits were emphasized. Traits such as fear, stress, and anxiety.

I attribute the failure to evolve to the concept of learned helplessness. Those who speak their minds—whether in-person or online—believe their problems are caused by someone else. We have the answers at our fingertips but throw our hands in the air and quit before we ever attempt to solve our problems. The instinct is to throw money at the problem, with apps to do it for us. Even worse, we distract ourselves away from the pain.

We are in the era of the most distractions, so it's also the most vital to learn how to focus and increase our attention spans.

How can we focus on ourselves and our effect on others around us? Take a moment of silence and check-in with your emotions. How are you feeling at this very moment? Do you enjoy this feeling? Why are you feeling this way?

So how can we increase our attention span? Proven methods involve observing our thoughts, what they concern, and where they derive from. Have you ever thought about something random and wondered where it came from? A sure-fire method to increase your attention span is to trace back the source of the thought as far as you can.

For instance, you are suddenly aware that you have no time and feel *overwhelmed*. Ask yourself, "why do you feel this way?" Like me, you probably started thinking about the dreaded *to-do list*—laundry, errands and deadlines. Perhaps you observe your inner voice saying, "there's not enough time in a day." As you trace further, you realize this thought isn't random at all. Your current task adds to this to-do list and by now you've named at least 10 things you haven't done. Now that you've arrived at the source of *overwhelm*, you can choose to take a breath and say, "there is time," before we act erratically and project our sense of overwhelm on those around us.

We are naturally curious beings. Be curious with your thoughts. Question their source. We are using our curiosity for things that don't matter—drama. Conversely, if we used it for things that did—us—we would evolve. We were born knowing how to observe others—that's our first instinct aside from eating and sleeping. As infants, we had to make sure our environment was safe. What we are not instinctively proficient in is—observing ourselves. We've been looking outward since the day we were born. It's time to look inward. We are easily aware of others behavior, but in order to be happy, we must begin to look at our own. It takes time, love and humility to develop this skill.

~

ON SCHOOL

I bring up school often because it's where we've spent most of our lives. It's where we spent the most vulnerable parts of our lives. Yet we are never taught practical life skills. Perhaps it's because our parents were supposed to supplement it.

In the modern era, however, I don't believe children spend quality time with their parents. Today, both parents typically work full-time. When children do see their parents, it's usually when parents are tired and already brain dead from the week. So I understand how the absence of supplemental life lessons occurred.

Children are left to spend a predominant amount of time at school. I don't understand why schools fail to offer practical life skills. I've heard the excuse that there's no money. Surprisingly, there is enough money to host free clinics for applying for

FASFA? Surprisingly, there are free after school programs in preparation for the SAT? Surprisingly, there are free clinics for creating your college application.? As you can see, I really disagree that there isn't money or time for schools to offer practical life skills.

Perhaps you think, "well maybe schools will overstep boundaries if their parents don't want them to learn specific ideas?" Schools are already pressuring children to choose careers and colleges. These are huge life decisions, yet we allow schools to make these for our children. What's the difference between teaching skills such as: how to develop healthy relationships, how to communicate or how to handle our emotions?

Why is there nothing in schools about alternative education? Schools merely promote one future path—college. What about the students who don't learn that way? What about students who don't want to be an employee for the rest of their lives? There is no promotion for trade schools, self-education, or creative avenues.

It's worth mentioning that it is mandatory to attend schools. If your parents do not send you to school, they can be fined and jailed. Schools need to evolve and become inclusive of all types of future avenues. If children spend most of their time in school, there should be classes or after school programs geared towards preparing them to navigate and be successful in life.

~

ON YOUTH

Children are products of learned and observed behavior. They learn from their peers in school. But children really emulate the behavior of adults. *Why?* Because we look up to them. We've spent our entire lives with them. They are our heroes. They are our role models.

I didn't know the term as a child, but I felt exactly what my parents were feeling. Now I realize, all that I felt was guilt, anger, regret, sadness, pain and unhappiness. Even though they said, "I believe in you," their actions said, "I'm starved, I'm alone, I'm afraid, run away." Some adults even say it out loud, "you don't want to grow up." Those adults are the ones who didn't learn how to grow up. *#I'mUpset* because no one gave us the full picture of how to grow up, and what it entailed. And this book is everything I can think of to express what it means to not only grow up but to Grow up and Prosper at it.

Adulthood is a liberating and beautiful experience. I believe the purpose of adolescence is to master our emotions. The purpose of adulthood is to share what we've learned. If we could become proficient in this, the coming generations would be better prepared.

Growing up is hard to do, but so was walking to our destination or riding a horse for ten days. If we have the technology to make our lives easier, of course, we are going to use it. That's innovation, that's forward-thinking, that's evolution. With progress comes happiness. We owe it to our future generations to be role models in growth, happiness and prosperity.

The youth watch our every move. They emulate our behaviors, beliefs and perceptions. They are extremely capable of understanding advanced topics. I commonly heard the cliché, "You're too young to understand." Are they? Every child I've talked too can understand. Every child I've talked to perfectly sees reality. Children only know Truth, they only know what they see. Children are capable. We do not give them the credit they deserve. We neglect their development and must begin to nurture it.

It's time for adults to step up to the plate. I don't care how tired you think you are. Take responsibility and grow!

~

ON INFLUENCE

We are massively influenced by that which we surround ourselves with. This includes the music we listen to, the videos we watch, the people we spend time with and the environment we live in. With social media alone, we are heavily advertised and marketed by companies. Whether we consciously know it or not, our decisions are heavily influenced by these marketing strategies.

These influences can be detrimental by causing unnecessary worry, fear or stress. Social media can cause anxiety, physical insecurities and addiction. We need to become aware of the ways these influences affect us. Music alone can subconsciously control the way we think, feel and act.

However, I am a strong proponent of *intentional influence*. I know that music and social media can provide inspiration, reliability, and emotional support.

It's important to develop discipline and awareness around such influences. It's important to develop discernment of the Truth rather than blind acceptance of whatever is said.

~

ON RELATIONSHIPS

As I've mentioned, the first relationship we participate in is with our family. However, we are never taught explicitly how to have healthy relationships. We are never taught what it takes to maintain one—what qualities are needed.

I've learned that communication is key to every relationship. You must be able to express your thoughts and emotions to one another. Before you can with each other, first, we must develop communication within. How do I even locate what my thoughts are? How do I identify my emotions? How can I express these in a way that is received and understood? The answer is—practice.

Ask yourself rhetorical questions such as: What am I thinking? How am I feeling? Imagine that your brain is a search engine. When you ask it a question, an answer is returned.

Our emotions are instinctive. The way we express our emotions requires refining. As infants, we communicate our emotions by yelling and crying. As children, we learn to use our words. It seems as adults, we go backward.

Perhaps then, we should implement Love. What is love? It's more than a physical connection. True love offers patience, kindness, understanding and compassion. True Love is unconditional and has no ulterior motive. Love does not expect anything in return. When we are failing to communicate and be heard, we can implement Love with ourselves. When we implement patience, we can encourage ourselves rather than condemn.

The most important key to every relationship is *growth*. Humans are cyclical but we also need variety. When both parties involved are concerned with growth, the relationship will flourish rather than become stagnant. Boredom will seldom arise.

A relationship is a compliment to what you already possess. If you are constantly relying on the relationship to fulfill a void within you, you will drain the relationship and it will suffer. Rather, contribute growth, love and gratitude which will energize the relationship.

~

ON SUCCESS

We are amid an era where you can spend your money faster than you can make it. And if you don't have any money—don't worry—use credit. Money is a means for survival, not a means for happiness. Do you have to pay your best friend to hang out with you? Your partner? Your children? Chances are you don't. It's been said that the best things in life are free. To which I strongly agree. I'm not saying, "quit your job and never make any money." I'm saying that money isn't the road to sustained happiness.

Money is merely one measurement of success. You can measure success by the level of happiness and fulfillment in your life. You can measure success by the quality of relationships you participate in. You can measure success by the ability to master one's emotions.

Money is merely a tool. Money is used as a means to an end. Money doesn't automatically bring happiness. It simply allows the chances of attaining happiness to increase. Although, it's not the only way to increase your chances of attaining happiness. *Of course, no one wants you to know that.*

What money really affords us in the modern world, is time. But if you have no idea how to use your time to cultivate things that actually bring you happiness, money is useless. If you sacrifice your relationships for money, you end up alone. Sure, you can buy fleeting moments of happiness. But that happiness is caused by external forces, rather than internal ones. Internal ones such as connection and alignment with the Self. Internal ones such as acceptance, courage, confidence and curiosity.

It's heavily portrayed in the modern culture that money equates success. It's heavily portrayed in the modern culture that money equates happiness. However, this could not be further from the truth. Success is unique to every individual. Success is set by each individual. It is not a one-size-fits-all phenomena.

Success can range from the development of Self to a fostering of animals. Success can range from attaining healthy relationships to creating art. Success can range from breaking a world record or creating the next crazed invention.

I believe success really is attained when our dreams match our reality. When we are what we think we are. When we practice what we preach. When we enjoy our lives and connect with others.

Success is relative. It's time for it to be common knowledge that success is beyond money.

~

ON STANDARDS

Once we leave our home we have the choice to keep, reject or refine the standards we've been taught. For some reason, it's unpopular to have high standards. Perhaps it's because it's correlated with exclusivity. Perhaps it's because standards such as status, money, looks or ethnicity were typically used.

It's not pompous to have high standards. It's not portrayed that standards can be a positive method for oneself. There are inclusive standards one can set. Such as honesty, responsibility, reliability and respect.

When we hold high standards of ourselves, others will recognize what we deserve. Standards are not meant to shame others who do not share similar standards. They are not meant to become the standards for everyone you meet. Like success, standards are relative. What one person values isn't the same for everyone. However, there are fundamental standards that individuals seeking happiness must adopt. As you begin to cultivate your native perspective, your standards will naturally rise.

~

These are a few brief topics that you can build upon to experience your native thoughts and beliefs. What parts mentioned resonated with you? Which parts did you disagree with? Perhaps you can take a few moments to begin on a topic of your choice. Perhaps it's your views of social media, influencers, religion, politics or sports. You will observe that you have a niche topic you predominately gravitate towards. This will shed light upon your unique qualities and native Self. When you begin to observe and record the topics of concern, it will bring you closer to your native Self. What do you think about? What are the native thoughts that frequent your mind?

On

I am predominately concerned with the way children develop and the effects on their efficacy throughout adulthood. I am concerned with the subtle but massive impact our environment plays in our lives. I am concerned with every way to live a balanced life and embrace your fullest potential.

CHAPTER 2

MANTRAS

Some call it affirmations,
Some call it incantations,

Others call it mantras,
but no matter the name,
the cause produced are one and the same.

You must affirm your native Self. You must repeat what is true. I've gathered the slogans and mantras I've repeated to myself countless times throughout my life. I live by these statements and am a proponent of their powers.

These mantras were my choruses—if you will—to keep me on track, like a song. They were a reminder of the reason why I was singing (living). The verses were the stories of my life. The choruses (mantras) all lead back to the main theme (me). Mantras are what shaped my standards and guided me on my journey to now.

> *Admittedly, I didn't put the name 'Mantra' to describe them until recent years when learning the term in my yoga teacher training.*

Some mantras are ones I created on my own. While others are ones I've heard and were inspired by. They're listed roughly in the order I've heard or created them. They're the progression of what led to my happiness. I've included relatively short explanations of each. Enjoy and take what resonates with you, leave what doesn't. Perhaps you create your own. Let's begin.

~

"KEEP MOVING FORWARD"

I heard this in *Meet the Robinsons,* a movie from my childhood. The quote derives from Walt Disney's original quote,

> *"We keep moving forward, opening new doors, and doing things because we're curious and curiosity keeps leading us down new paths."*

Keep Moving Forward inspired me to never give up and never lose hope; To let it go and grow. The movie promoted a culture of celebrating failures. I feel that in our modern society many fear failure. But in my life, I've learned that failure is what makes us great. The key is that when we fail, we choose to keep moving forward. And it's not to say that we ignore why we failed. We analyze what went wrong, learn from it, implement the change, and try again!

~

"JUST DO IT!"

I've been involved in sports since I can remember. After all, I learned to ride a dirt bike before a regular bike—I have pictures to prove it!

Since 1988, the shoe company, Nike, promoted the slogan, *Just Do It!* Similar to The Home Depot's more recent slogan, *Let's Do This.*

I'd say the nature of these "mantras" was hidden and in the background of my life. Anytime I stepped onto the field, into the gym or grabbed my bag, the mantra repeated itself to me.

Just Do It, promoted fearless achievement. It denied hesitation and evoked action. These are my core values, that when applied in my life, has brought me the most happiness. Although there were many moments of failure, it was the moments I felt most alive.

~

IT'S WORTH IT

This is one of my own mantras. I used this phrase whenever I was in doubt. When I questioned my ability or when I felt insecure. After debating with myself internally, I would use this as a power move—if you will—to convince myself to take action. When you realize that you must make a choice, you must convince yourself it's worth it to act upon it, otherwise, any ounce of doubt will catastrophize[3] your outcome. I committed 100% of myself when I repeated this mantra. *It's worth it,* provided me the energy I didn't think I had some days. It hasn't failed me yet. It evokes complete confidence in my decision that I deliver full force.

~

---

[3] I know that's not a word, but remember I said I was going to make up my own? I could've used jeopardize but I didn't haha

"MAKE IT A GREAT DAY OR NOT, THE CHOICE IS YOURS"

I was roughly eight years old, in third grade. I distinctly remember hearing this quote every day after the morning announcements in elementary school. Whether or not I consciously knew it then—for the remainder of that year—I felt responsible for the outcome of my day.

Of course, I didn't recognize the impact it made until recently. The repetitive nature of this quote contributed to my belief that we control the emotional outcome of our day. Sure, I may not be able to physically control what occurs, but I can choose the way it affects me. My perception of a *great* day depends solely on my mindset.

Whenever I had a perceived *bad* day, I thought of this quote and made it my mantra to turn the day around. This mantra challenged me to find the positive side. I hesitate to use the word *always*, but I am most *certain* despite the *bad* day when I repeated this mantra, I found some lesson to learn from it.

This simple mantra evoked a sense of accomplishment rather than failure. I also take accountability for choosing to put my best foot forward when utilizing this mantra.

A prayer that explains this quote well goes:

God Grant Me the Serenity
To Accept the Things I Cannot Change
The Courage to Change the Things I Can
And the Wisdom To Know the Difference

I'm going to do everything in my power to chose to have a great day, but if things still go sideways I will accept it, and still have a great day because it was a day of learning and growth.

> *aside*—The fact that I had to dissect my childhood for clues of what led me to now is what *#I'mUpset* about. Who really has the time and energy to do this? Why couldn't we merely support all child dreams from the outset? It would mitigate the time it takes to unravel the depths of suppressed consciousness.

~

"PUT YOURSELF IN THEIR SHOES, HOW WOULD YOU FEEL IF YOU WERE IN THEIR SHOES"

I'm uncertain of when and what brought this mantra about. What I am certain of—my father told my brother and me this mantra very often. I suppose the nature he intended for us was not to take toys that didn't belong to us.

Naturally, I took this to heart, as it became every essence of who I am. I applied this in as many emotional situations that I could. I never wanted anyone to ever feel pain, hurt or isolation. Although I didn't always respond in the best ways, I did try my best, with the knowledge I had at the time.

This mantra taught me perspective and respect. To this day, I truly dedicate my heart space to become an unbiased observer and honor the perspective of another. I put my emotions, intellect and ego aside so that I can immerse myself in the perspective of another.

I've found that when I repeat this mantra, I immediately come from a place of love. It shifts my emotions to seek to understand, rather than seek to disprove or attack. I've also found that when I live in their shoes from a place of love, often I find positive resolutions to the matter at hand.

~

I'LL GET OUT

I remember eight years old very well, it was a big year. I got my first pet—which is still alive today—I moved to a new house, started at a new school, began writing songs, got my first and only guitar, started walking home from school, and started remembering the details of all the arguments my parents had. Alas, the inception of *I'll Get Out*.

This mantra served me well—it served me a very long time. It seems it was the only mantra I had from eight to eighteen years old; mostly because I can't remember a time my parents weren't arguing.

I'd save all my money, and at times when I'd be hurt the most, I'd plan my escape, I'd plan to run away. The most I remember saving was $500.

But I never ran away. I never went through with it. I always talked myself out. I usually scared myself out of it. I'd ask myself, "Where would you go anyway? What if the police picked you up? Worse, what if you got kidnapped?" I'd scare myself, "When your parents find you, they're going to send you off to a military camp or prep school. You'll lose all your freedom. They'll send you to a psychiatrist. You'll be forced to take medicine." I'd continue the thought process with, "But I am sane, I am a good student, I will be successful in life, I don't want my freedom taken away."

So I decided I'd be better off if I stayed home, did well in school, kept my freedom, left for college, then I'd be free. So throughout my adolescent period, I'd always say subconsciously, "I'll get out."

During sports—although I did enjoy it—in the moments of silence, I knew it was simply a stepping-stone for me to leave one day and never look back. When I saved money from babysitting, birthdays, selling candy at school, jobs, washing cars, washing and walking dogs (long before *Wag*[4]) I knew it was all for the plan to get out. I knew paying attention in school—although I did enjoy it—was all part of the plan. Keep my sanity, keep my freedom, leave.

So if you're reading this now, it means this mantra did its job. It kept me on target for my goal. I did make it out. Fortunately, I made it out with more than simply my freedom. I made it out, happy.

~

IF YOU WAKE UP TOMORROW AND STILL FEEL THIS WAY, GO-AHEAD

This wasn't a positive mantra. It was a survival mantra. But a mantra worth mentioning; because I repeated it nearly every night for two years straight between the ages of fourteen and sixteen. Sometimes, I'd repeat it on my loneliest days prior or after those ages, but those two years in particular. Despite my, *I'll get out* mantra, sometimes it wasn't empowering enough. Sometimes I felt like quitting, rather than trying to get out. As I

---

[4] A company that provides dog walking services

write this next sentence, please hear it as genuine transparency, rather than a cry for help or pity.

I was silently suicidal. I never shared this, because of my fear to get thrown into a mental asylum or be drugged out of sanity. But I contemplated it nearly every night. I went over every possible way in my head, came close a few times, but repeated this mantra and talked myself out of it.

When I repeated this mantra, a rush of other thoughts came to mind, without effort, "You'll hurt your parents, you'll bring shame to the family name, who would even care anyway, it wouldn't matter if you did or didn't. The only way it would matter is if sometime in the future you were happy, and you were robbing your present self of that experience. I desperately crave happiness. I experience fleeting moments of happiness and hope, wouldn't it feel amazing if I could feel that all the time? I don't know how right now, but it has to be possible, right?"

After my attempts to convince myself out of it, the helplessness would creep back. I'd be exhausted from the inner dialogue, from the tears, from the pain. So once more I repeated, "well Toni, If you wake up tomorrow, and still feel this way, go-ahead."

Fortunately, every morning I woke up. It didn't hurt so bad. My level of emotions was less. I felt like I could bear to stay another day. Did the emotions go away? Did my body in sleep reset them? Or did I internalize and bury them deep within my subconscious? Perhaps you may already know the answer. Again, I'm sharing the *progression* of mantras that **led** to my happiness, not immediately produced happiness. And this mantra, left me in survival mode until I would finally *get out*.

~

NO MATTER HOW BAD IT IS OR HOW BAD IT GETS I AM GOING TO MAKE IT

While in autopilot, the only things I paid attention to in high school were necessities. It was necessary for me to get into college. I became proficient in everything college acceptance entailed. I excelled in grades. I participated in sports. I worked an hourly job.

It was also necessary for me to stay alive. I paid attention to any tactics, strategies, or significant things that could contribute to my well-being—the rest I ignored. Later we will find out, I merely suppressed the rest, and created my own GAD, PTSD and Social Anxiety.

Of course, not all plans go accordingly, I was hypnotized by a boy in my class, but that's another topic for a later time.

I digress, so I repeated this mantra to remind myself— while doing the necessary tasks involved with college acceptance and survival—I can make it.

~

GET OUT OF YOUR MIND!

If you haven't noticed already, I'm a thinker. An obsessive thinker in the least. Sometimes I'd catch myself so deep in thought, that I neglected my best friend. As I've shared, a boy mesmerized me. I was so focused on getting out and surviving, that when I saw him for the first time, my heart gravitated towards his.

Serendipitously, we fell in love. Many moments, my best friend would eagerly connect with me, I found myself wanting to share, but hesitating for the survival and for the sake of my uneasy heart. I didn't have to repeat this mantra very often because in almost every interaction I willingly, without hesitation, exposed my true being to him.

The times I did repeat this, however, is when we'd have breakups and the only way to save us, was to divulge every emotion and thought I could ever hold back. I'd yell at myself, "Get Out Of Your Mind!" to get everything out, because I knew if we ended, and there was an ounce of something I could've said, and I didn't say it, I would be devastated.

~

WHY NOT

Of course, there are tons of specific mantras tailored to our relationship throughout high school, but I'd ruin our next book. So I'll continue with my personal, individual mantras that contributed to my current happiness today.

This next mantra occurred as I approached my life long goal, *to get out!* I was accepted to college. I could feel my heart vibrating.

Why Not promoted a carefree attitude. I was thrilled that the years of practice turned into days until freedom alas. From simply survival to newfound freedom, I expanded my thoughts to, "Why not be successful, why not be happy, live life, be free, do what I want, be who I want?"

I celebrated silently, to have conquered my life's goal to date.

~

EXPAND YOUR MIND

"Open yourself to perspective, possibilities and opportunities," I told myself as I left for college. "You are finally out, be free, and live your life. Expand Your Mind."

~

"WHO YOU SURROUND YOURSELF WITH YOU BECOME"

My carefree attitude led me to the massive opportunity of possibility. With the diploma in one hand, acceptance letter in the other, I confidently said yes to discovering all that life had to offer me.

Barely a month after graduation, I attended a seminar for a multi-level marketing company.

> *I'd say it's a rite of passage for all young adults in the modern-day era to be apart of some type of marketing model.*

The seminar was really for personal development now that I reflect back. The premise, "how can you sell someone a product when you can't even sell you on yourself?" Long story short, at this seminar, a speaker's—of whom I don't recall their name—words of advice were, "Who you surround yourself with, you become."

They suggested that if our group of friends wasn't goal-oriented, then we would become unmotivated and decrease our odds of a successful future. At the time, I'd never heard such concepts before. I was moved, to say the least. If my friends weren't who I wanted to become, then I need to start hanging around people I did want to become. But first I had to answer, "Well who do I want to be?"

~

I'M NOT GOING TO FAIL. I DON'T KNOW WHAT IT IS OR WHAT I'M GOING TO DO YET, BUT I'M NOT GOING TO FAIL

This mantra is kind of reminiscent of, "No matter how bad it is, or how bad it gets, I am going to make it." Except that this mantra alludes that I have no idea what the path is. I don't know where the hell I'm going. All I know is that when I do find out—whatever it is—I will not fail in it. This mantra encouraged my pursuit to discover who I was.

~

EXPLORE DARKNESS EMBRACE SILENCE

Here I am, open to opportunity. Confident I will excel and free more than ever. So I said yes to a free workshop offered on campus. I uncovered this mantra myself while meditating for the first time. As I closed my eyes, a projection of visions unfolded. I ventured into my thoughts and experienced the vast fluidity of them. It was as if a cork had been pulled off a bottle, I was immersed in my being. There, in the depths, I heard a whisper from a familiar voice, "Explore Darkness & Embrace Silence."

> *At this point, you may be saying to yourself, "Okay, Toni, you're walking off the edge, you've lost me." Fear not, let me explain.*

Let's tackle the first part, "Explore Darkness." It means that I won't be afraid to traverse the depths of darkness within and around me. Darkness represents all that is unknown to me. Darkness is not associated with evil, in this instance, but merely the unfamiliar thoughts and emotions that were unknowingly there all along. This mantra was an imperative statement that commanded I continue further on this journey within.

The second part, "Embrace Silence," served as a reassurance of safety and security. Although I had never meditated before, I told myself I'd be safe to explore alone. That I will embrace the silence of the journey, to continue to meditate, through the emotions and thoughts observed and unearthed.

~

"#MAKEMOVES"

Admittedly, I did not meditate long before taking a hiatus from it. I had unearthed years of subconscious thoughts, emotions and memories. I remember consciously saying to myself, "You have tons of things to address, so take a break from meditating and start handling the dilemmas at hand."

Naturally, I was overwhelmed by all these thoughts I hadn't paid any attention to. I caught myself falling into depression again. So on January 18, 2016, I promised myself that I **WILL** *genuinely* smile again. I asked myself, "Why the hell are you depressed, love? You made it out of the house, you should be excited!"

That's when I realized I *was* making moves. But moves that were for the fake *Toni*—the *Toni* I needed to let go of. I had to throw that away and accept my True Self. Though, I didn't know what that was yet. I needed to make moves for *Toni*. A lyric from J. Cole comes to mind, "Good news is [*Toni*] you came a long way, bad news is [*Toni*] you went the wrong way."

I might have wasted time I could've spent on developing my creativity, but it was all part of the process, and not to fret, *now* I can focus on developing it. Hence, mantra *#MakeMoves*. Moves toward the real Toni. The Toni, who I later found out, was creative, artistic, loving and more.

~

"YOU AIN'T GETTING ANY YOUNGER"
-SEINABO SEY

Mantras are a reminder to stay the course of my life goals. But if you don't use the mantra, you lose the reminder.

I was in college, so of course, I got distracted—no rules, no supervision. I stopped repeating mantras to myself. I found myself way off track, getting into bad habits that really *really* wasted time and didn't contribute to making moves towards the real Toni.

Until I heard the song *Younger (Remix) by Kygo (Seinabo Sey)* which became my new mantra to get me back on track. It reminded me that I'm getting older by the minute. If I don't act now, I'll run out of time! There's nothing more motivating than remembering you're going to die one day!

~

DON'T WAIT UNTIL ITS TOO LATE - REALIZATION, IT'S NEVER TOO LATE

So I refueled for the trek into myself. We all know it's never that easy. It may be simple, but not easy. My fears crawled out. I began to succumb to self-doubt. I experienced feelings that I, "missed the boat," so to speak, to be the real me. Here I am, the first four quarters of college completed. I thought of switching majors from Chemistry, to Biology, to Philosophy, to Public Health, to English! *What?* Inside I knew neither one of them would suffice. But my inner voice wouldn't let me give up on the path to me. So I repeated, "Don't wait until it's too late, Toni, it's never too late, you still have time, do the unthinkable!" And as you've read, I decided to drop out of college completely.

~

I OWE ME LIFE

Of course, I was in the middle of the fall quarter. So I thought it best to at least finish out before leaving. Once my mind accepted the end of college, I ran wild inside. And with that, the inception of *I Owe Me Life*.

Traditionally the saying goes, "I owe you." In this case, *I Owe Me Life* was a convincing tool to stand for what I deserve. I declared that, "I owe myself happiness, love, confidence, fulfillment, dreams, and more."

This mantra inspired me to take action for goals that were conducive to my core values. I became obsessed with living a balanced life. The sub-mantra—if you will—is doing anything that led to becoming physically fit, mentally strong, emotionally stable and spiritually well.

This mantra encouraged me to raise my standards for my life and not settle for anything less than. *I Owe Me Life* was the gateway mantra to say goodbye to a life of survival and hello to a life of prosperity.

~

PROLONG THE INEVITABLE PREPARE FOR THE EVITABLE

I knew I had some demons I've been ignoring. I knew it was time to face them. They were only going to keep coming back. I openly admit *dedicating your life intentionally to balance is a huge endeavor.* Physical fitness was straightforward. The latter three required patience, unconditional love and constant reflection with oneself. To truly become balanced, I needed to surrender to my past.

I told myself, "If I don't face this now, I will only prolong the inevitable, I must prepare for the evitable." Time and time again, life shows me that when you simply ignore emotions, they come back with greater dismay; greater intensity.

Life—in general—occurs in this manner. When we ignore important moments, they come back to bite us. I'm certain we all remember a time when procrastination led to greater pain than simply handling the situation at its inception. So I repeated this mantra to cheer me on while unearthing all the mental, emotional and spiritual pain inside.

~

"DOUBTS ARE NOT REAL; THEY ARE ILLUSIONS CREATED TO KEEP US FROM TAKING RISKS BECAUSE WE ARE AFRAID TO FAIL"

This was a quote from *Journey Into Power*. It inspired me to overcome my fears in the pursuit of rediscovering my true self. I thought to myself, "Ok Toni, you're on the path to healing, let's start building that future of happiness now." I began to take massive risks in finding a career path that would fit my needs. I explored careers I was most familiar with first—fitness.

~

GET STIMULATED

I found myself in the shower one day—where all great ideas and epiphanies come from. I realized I got bored and unproductive again. I *fell off* again and decided the cure was to *Get Stimulated*, I've dedicated an entire chapter to this concept and will expand more there.

Spoiler alert: it's one of my most powerful mantras.

~

EVERY FAILURE IS ONE STEP CLOSER TO SUCCESS

I tried new career paths of wellness, but I still wasn't getting the sustainable happiness I craved. Instead of giving up, I told myself I'm one step closer to finding the right career for me. I embraced the path to progress. My perspective shifted from failure to gratitude. I was thankful to cross one more thing off the list that wasn't truly me.

Sure I loved all the ways that could bring physical fitness to people, but I no longer enjoyed doing it. It turns out, fitness wasn't enough variety for me.

COMPARISON IS THE THIEF OF JOY

At some point we all catch up to each other, so don't worry where anyone else is. I found myself, a college drop out, with nothing to show for. Internally, I had grown massively but on paper, I had been in the same spot for the last two years.

Social media contributed heavily to my sadness and self-doubt. I am imperfect, despite my path to spread wellness, I'd log on and see everyone, "doing it big." I felt behind. Then I heard the quote, "Comparison is the thief of joy." I immediately connected to it and made it my daily mantra when I found myself criticizing my progress.

This spontaneous urgency to compete with others' progress ruined the results of my path. I truly enjoy this path I'm on. It isn't the easiest to measure the progress, but it's there I assure you. When I spent time comparing myself to others, the joy left instantly from my daily work. I felt forced to, "do more, go faster." I know we compare for competition, significance and pace, but the best competition is within yourself. Because if you compete with yourself, you'll have challenges for a lifetime. You'll also limit your excuses for why things went wrong. You are the reason it went wrong, now get back out there and fix it.

LIVE LIFE INTENTIONALLY

I was taking a yoga class one day when I thought of this mantra. I traced back my thoughts and realized it came from this inner dialogue:

> "What are you living life for? What do you want out of your one and only life? I don't want to go through life I want to GROW through life. I don't want life to just happen to me. I want to be an active participant. There are many things I want that won't simply, fall into my lap. I must go out and create the life I deserve!"

This mantra reminds me to be intentional with my life. To also live life consciously. To carry myself in a way that is conducive to my standards. If you're not going to participate in your life, who is?

~

YOU DON'T HAVE TO BE A PROFESSIONAL TO BE HAPPY IN LIFE

When I left high school, I had the mindset that I needed to have a college degree and career to be happy. I realized I don't. Not that there's anything wrong with it, but college and a typical career just wasn't for me.

I'm an artist, I'm an entrepreneur. I have a very free spirit. I enjoy creating my schedule and have the discipline to follow it. I like variety and spontaneity; I felt these qualities had a stigma to them growing up.

I felt guilty for dropping out. I felt I didn't deserve success. I call it the, *"withdrawals from the traditional mindset."* I was going through change in the most direct way: elimination, isolation and deprivation. I followed the traditional mindset my entire life. Now, when I declare I am worthy of more, I experienced conflictions. Conflictions, of a life I was taught to live rather than a life that I was *meant* to live.

I had to surrender to the typical conventions of what I was told equated happiness. I had to replace the mindset with my natural one. I told myself, "It's part of the process, when I'm sober I'll be happier."

~

DON'T CRY OVER SPILLED MILK

I've wasted too much time obsessing over what went wrong. I healed significantly faster when I allowed myself to mope. When I embraced my emotions and let go of the emotional charge. When I admitted what went wrong, changed it, and tried again. The best way to get over failure is to follow up with huge success. So when I do fail, I modify and try again as quickly as possible. It happened already. I can't waste more time drowning in self-pity. I need to direct all my energy towards fixing, improving and being successful! *Don't cry over spilled milk*, in other words, learn from the mistakes, improve them and try again!

Tony Robbins says it better,

> *"Life is Happening FOR Us, not To Us...Even the problems are gifts. If we learn from them."*

~

DON'T STRESS OVER PEOPLE IN YOUR PAST. THERE'S A REASON THEY DIDN'T MAKE IT TO YOUR FUTURE

I believed in the message *I Owe Me Life* so much. It was heartbreaking when I couldn't communicate it to the ones I loved most. I was obsessed with living a happy life because I saw all their unhappiness growing up. I'd worked so hard on myself over the past three years. I desperately wanted them to find the joy I had found in my life. I'd literally buzz with excitement for reaching the expansion and growth in my life.

The path to your dreams is a lonely road. Many entrepreneurs have repeated that the road to success is a lonely one. And when I heard this quote, I made it my mantra immediately.

I realized it's not a lonely road because the people who are meant to be there with you, are still there. I stopped focusing on all the people I was losing and started focusing on all the ones still along for the ride.

It wasn't an easy mantra to follow. I even lost some family members for a while. If you can't tell already, I'm a very direct communicator. Often people don't want or are ready to hear the truth. I'm an *empath,* so I'm highly sensitive to others emotions. I truly immerse myself in the shoes of others. I'm a friend that will always do whatever they can to be supportive. But I reach a point where I cannot take the pain anymore. I can't stand by and watch someone be hurt by someone else, or even worse, hurt themselves. I can't beat myself up about why we don't hang out anymore. I can send them love from a distance. And I can repeat, "Don't stress over people in your past, there's a reason they didn't make it to your future."

~

TRUST THE PROCESS

I question myself quite often, "Am I on the right path? Am I flowing with ease, or forcing certain situations? Forcing goals that aren't truly me? I don't feel excited." I begin questioning myself more than ever. *What's the cure?* Repeat the mantra, *"Trust the Process."*

When I take an active role in my life, I get signs that what I'm doing is part of the process. I'll have breakthroughs with myself and with those closest to me. So I keep on keeping on. I learn to trust the process. Soon I began to enjoy the process too.

~

WHY GET MAD AT YOURSELF IF YOU NEVER KNEW

Often, I'm overly harsh on myself. I tell my friends, "I'm a type A personality with my goals, type B with my lifestyle." Anything derivative from my *type a* side, I slam myself with ridicule for why I didn't figure things out faster. I guilt myself, "Why didn't you avoid mistakes altogether, or take action sooner?" Then I remind myself to *trust the process*, be kind, loving and patient with myself. It's true, why get mad at myself if I didn't know, like Biggie said, *"if [I] don't know, now [I] know."*

GET OUT OF YOUR HEAD AND INTO YOUR HEART

At this point, I'm becoming fully happy within. Now it's time to make my internal happiness match the external world. I've spent the past few years developing a career that I loved. I applied any techniques of productivity to fast track my success. But I realized the more I forced progress, the more inauthentic I felt. So I decided to always come from a place of love, just as I had been so successful within. My progress in my career elevated quickly, and soon I found out that my internal and external world could become one. This led to the inception of my new mantra.

~

MAKE LOVE YOUR LIFE

I've sought to expand on the initial mantra, "Make it a great day or not the choice is yours." When you *make love your life,* every day is truly a great day. With love, you do things without condition, without expectation, with patience, with understanding and with gratitude. I am enacting my choice. My choice to love. By loving I am making my day great.

When I repeated this mantra, I tapped into an eternal source of energy and light. I'd realized when I Made Love My Life, in all that I do, everything flowed effortlessly—successfully.

I'm sure you've heard, "love your life." But that didn't carry enough *umphh*—if you will. *Make Love Your Life*, does. When you add "make" the whole picture changes, from gratitude to intention! *Live life intentionally!* Life doesn't happen to you, it happens for you!

Adding "make" shows you have control. You have a choice! It's an entirely new meaning.

> *I'd like to share my realization from a post on April 10, 2019.*

> *My new mantra for year 22!*
> *"Make Love Your Life"*
> *Thank you for all the birthday wishes! This year will be the best year yet! Full of blessings, love, friends, family, and adventure! I remember when I was in third grade, every morning the principal would end the morning announcements with this quote, "Make it a great day or not, the choice is yours." And now at 22, I've come to truly grasp this significance. I have the power of choice, and in most instances, the power of control...and...if I choose love; If I make love an essential part of my day to day life, then every day, will truly be, a great day.*
> *At 18, my mantra was, "Explore Darkness and Embrace Silence."*

I had just moved out, and I was ready to conquer the world! And 4 short years later, I'm feeling beyond content; Happy, Blessed...Surrounded by the most AMAZING people, and creating the Life of Love, I was so longing for. What is love? It's simple, and 1 Corinthians 13:4-7 says it best; Love is simple, but here's the catch, it's not easy! It's not easy to be patient, kind, truthful, to make sacrifices, to be vulnerable. But it is possible! And think I've found it! Cheers to the best year yet!

~

DO WHAT YOU LOVE ENJOY WHAT YOU DO

This is a very recent mantra, within the last few months leading up to the release of this very book. I haven't had much time to dissect it. All I know, is that after repeating all these other mantras for the past fourteen years of my life, this mantra **instantly** changes my mood. It makes the decision process effortless. Simplified in every way. This mantra is a defeater of doubt—mother of all motivators.

~

As you can see, the recurring cycle of my life consisted of inspired, action-filled moments, followed by massive self-doubt. I experienced moments of complacency, where I was unhappy, but not unhappy enough to change. I experienced heavy internal dialogue.

Mantras were simply one strategy to pull me out and set me back on the path to my happiness.

The repetition of these mantras contributed to my happiness. To date, I've chosen to integrate the two most impactful ones together—Make Love Your Life & Do What You Love, Enjoy What You Do.

I encourage you to find some positive ones that fit you. Repeat them daily—as a reminder of who you are and what you're about—to keep you on track. Often times there are negative mantras we say to ourselves, perhaps think about the ones you repeat daily, and replace them with encouraging ones instead.

Some of my old ones included, "I'm not good enough, nobody will listen, I don't deserve happiness, I am not worthy of love." Eliminate the negative self-talk and witness your mood and productivity skyrocket.

Mantras are a proven method for me to encourage myself when I feel discouraged. These mantras inspired me in times of doubt, they empowered me in moments of depression. These are the powers of mantras. As a refined personal definition, mantras are reminders of who I am, who I will be and what I'm worth. I repeated mantras of my standards, and I knew I'd never settle for anything less.

Take a moment to check-in with yourself. How are you feeling? Can you write down a few mantras you say to yourself?

PART II

Establish Trust: Align Mind & Body

Chapter 3

SPIRITUAL ENTREPRENEUR

"Drive Thy Business or It Will Drive Thee"
—*Benjamin Franklin*

You must embrace who you are. This is the simplest way to establish trust between the mind and body. Prove to your mind that your heart can evolve.

When you own your vocation, you feel like you're on vacation. When you don't embrace who you are, often, you're filled with hatred, anguish, pain, guilt, shame and suffering.

~

For what seemed like forever, I couldn't find the career path that fulfilled all my needs. I couldn't find sustained happiness. I knew the lifestyle I wanted. One that was flexible, fluid, diverse and spontaneous. One that allowed me to set my schedule. All directions pointed towards entrepreneurship.

Unfortunately, I had associated entrepreneurship with money-hungry individuals. Those ready to do whatever it took to be on top. My confusion stemmed from movies and society's ideas that negatively portrayed the rich.

Money is a sore subject for me because it's all my parents ever argued about. Here, I have a viable pathway that fits my lifestyle but it conflicts with my morals—*Never take advantage of somebody or take their money in exchange for a product that didn't help them.* So, I looked toward a true entrepreneur, Sir Richard Branson—a billionaire who created Virgin Airlines—for his definition which states, "Being an entrepreneur simply means being someone who wants to make a difference in other people's lives." There's also an entire specific niche called, "Spiritual Entrepreneurship." According to Damien Wills, "spiritual entrepreneurs only create products or services that benefit and inspire humanity." *I can vibe with that all day.*

~

Okay, great so that solves one problem, but what about my sustained happiness? I finally realized it wasn't the job I had unhappiness with. It was me. I was ready for more than merely a survival mode lifestyle. There were still unresolved pieces of my past. I wanted to be happy, but first I needed to heal. With my limited relationship with success, I took to the only way I'd experienced success—I implemented entrepreneurial methods.

Although unconventional, I decided to apply the same essence to my own life. I began to see my life as a business. A legitimate business whose purpose is to fulfill a need in return for compensation. After all,

> *"The [Greatest] investment you can make,*
> *is in yourself."*
> *-Warren Buffet.*

I thought to myself, "If I want my business to grow, I must grow. If I want my business to prosper, I must flourish. If I want my business to be useful, I must obsess over avenues of utility."

After a few years of applying this 5-Step Method, I became successful in my business—my life. I grew inward. I grew in my relationships. I grew in my capacity for love. I am happy. I am shaping into everything I am, everything I deserve. I am unapologetically me. What I have is something you cannot touch. But it is something that can sustain you for your entire life. It is love, perseverance, acceptance, courage, humility, trust and divine flow. You need You. In this world today that tells us we need to have more things to be happy, it's a very powerful thing to have. Being You, in the truest, most genuine form is a very liberating and peaceful experience.

The shackles are off, today, tomorrow, and for the rest of my life.

~

So what is this 5-Step Method?

Employ The Entrepreneurial Process

1. Adopt the Right Mindset
2. Take Action
3. Be Resourceful
4. Keep Record
5. Repeat, Reject or Refine

STEP 1: ADOPT THE RIGHT MINDSET

In general, the mindset of an entrepreneur is solely success based. We do anything and everything that it takes to reach our goals—legally and ethically, of course. We are relentless and obsessive. The simple premise of an entrepreneur is, "If I don't know, I'm gonna figure it out. If that means I have to educate myself, if that means I have to hire somebody else, if that means I have to change, I will."

Whatever your goal is, you must come from a frame of mind to never give up and keep moving forward. That being said, let's establish what your goal is. Let's establish your mission statement—*the reason Life is in business*.

Imagine your Life as a real business. A legitimate business whose purpose is to serve a need in return for compensation. Imagine here, that the compensation is happiness. The purpose of your business (life) is to serve your needs in return for happiness. Ok, read it again, this time substitute *your* with *my*.

The purpose of my life is to serve my needs in return for happiness.

This is your mission statement. Make it clear and concise. Adjust if necessary.

~

STEP 2: TAKE ACTION

You must take action to serve all your needs. And you'll need to cultivate a set of qualities to do so. In general, entrepreneurs can plan, execute and evolve. We are also disciplined and agile. Entrepreneurs are organized, committed, self-reliant and consistent. Above all, entrepreneurs adapt.

Each of these qualities you **must** excel in if you wish to stay in business. Do you want to know a secret? You already possess all these qualities! Perhaps some are stronger than others, but it's simply because you haven't been using them! If you don't utilize things, what do they do? *Wither away.* All you must do is practice. Practice and love yourself along the way.

With these qualities, you will be driven to involve yourself with anything that can serve your needs. In order to be happy, you must heal from whatever caused the unhappiness. Start immersing yourself in whatever ways you know to heal. This book can be one of them. Think of the ways you already know of.

You also must grow. What are some ways you know to grow? So, in short, take action to achieve the life you deserve and as you take action, practice the qualities of an entrepreneur. You are the entrepreneur. Your business is your life!

~

STEP 3: BE RESOURCEFUL

If nothing is working, you must be resourceful! Go out and find more ways to fulfill your needs. You're already killing it because reading books is a phenomenal way to stimulate your mind and open more doors to opportunity. Another great tool I used frequently, was an app called *Groupon*. You don't know what you don't know until you try! It's where I found Yoga and unlocked an entirely spiritual side of me I didn't know was there! I also bought an *Intro To Pottery* class, which stimulated my artistic side.

In short, refrain from using the term, "I did my best." If you feel like quitting. *Why?* Because how can you do your best, if you're simply trying the same methods you always have—that are clearly not working? It's time to get new methods, and the only way to find them is to be resourceful! Don't wait for the perfect time to begin walking a conscious pathway towards happiness. Go out and create the perfect environment. Get curious, get hungry!

~

STEP 4: KEEP RECORD

Keep track of your progress by writing everything down! Not only is it a great tool for growth, but it's also therapeutic! This very book is a composition of all my progress in the last four years. You never know what will come of it! Since you are a business, keep a log of your yearly, quarterly, and monthly progress. Write all your goals down. Write any epiphanies, breakthroughs, emotions and thoughts that arise as your journey to You. Every so often, check-in. See where you are at, where you've come, and where you are headed. You can vary your record on your phone, laptop, voice memos or anywhere else. Try to stay consistent. I recommend a place that can be recovered easily in one, safe place.

~

STEP 5: REPEAT, REJECT OR REFINE

This is where record-keeping comes into play. What strategies have been working? Which haven't? What are some ways you can adjust and refine so that they are successful? After going through steps 1-4, you've gathered enough data to do your first assessment. During your first assessment, ask yourself the previous questions. Then, choose to Repeat, Reject or Refine your methods. I've included a short description of each choice. Choose the one that best fits the method you are assessing.

Repeat—If it ain't broke don't fix it. Simplicity is key. Even an inch of progress is still progress. If you find yourself getting more and more uncomfortable, that is a true sign of growth.

> *"In order to have what you've never had you must do what you've never done."*
> *-Thomas Jefferson*

Stay the course. Keep the same mindset. Repeat your actions. Repeat your methods of resourcefulness. Continue keeping a record of whichever methods you choose!

Reject—If you're going backward, it's time to revisit your methods of choice. If you're finding yourself unmotivated or stuck, you need to change your approach. Remember the qualities of an entrepreneur. Make a new plan, find new strategies to execute it, get stimulated and grow!

> *A side note:* Think of your habits and emotions as your employees. If they're not doing a good job, you must fire them. Perhaps the habits you currently possess are interfering with your progress. Take responsibility in answering truthfully about which habits are conducive to your mission statement. Eliminate habits that do not serve your goals. Also, particular emotions are sometimes detrimental to our goals. When I put myself down, I become complacent. Again, truthfully ask yourself and become mindful of whether or not the emotions are contributing to your goals.

Refine—If you're finding any inch of progress; mentally, physically, emotionally or spiritually, perhaps all you need is a little tweak. Perhaps your action and resourcefulness is excelling, but your mindset is holding you back. This is where practice comes into play. You'll start to develop a subtle awareness—an instinct—of noticing what works well with you.

~

As you find success and become well versed in these steps, I urge you to isolate each new tactic. For example, you change one specific mindset, keep everything the same and continue through the steps. This is for the ultimate refining process once you have the momentum of success and simply need to fine-tune it.

Take a moment to write down your mission statement if you haven't already. Simplicity is key. Grab any notebook and dedicate it to your journey ahead. Daily read aloud your mission statement. If you feel safe, share with trusted others so that it will hold you accountable. This will help you stay committed to your pathway to happiness. Y

ou've been in business since the day you were born, it's time to live the life you deserve. You are worthy of healing. You are worthy of growth. You are worthy of happiness. You are not willing to settle for anything less. When you push past your threshold of comfort, liberation awaits you on the other side.

Chapter 4

GET STIMULATED

"You can't go back and change the beginning but you can start where you are and change the ending."
—C.S. Lewis

You must grow. This requires a change of habit. Your dedication to the evolution of your heart earns the minds trust.

Life is too short to spend it doing things you don't love, for people who don't care about you. Life is too short to spend it distracted from your True self. Life is too short to live anything less than what you deserve. My first life goal was to get out, then it was to live a life I deserve. The byproduct of this goal happened to be happiness.

The truth is, you don't *find* happiness, you create it within. It's not some far off place you have to have a million dollars, the perfect career or the perfect life to visit. It's right here, right now. It's simply a matter of choice. In my life, I am happy when I accept who I am, do what I love, enjoy what I do and share it with the ones I care about. Perhaps it's useful to revisit the list you created on what makes you happy.

The proven method for me to attain happiness is to *grow*. Grow to accept who I am, dare to fulfill my dreams, expand myself for the sake of humanity. When I am my highest self, I can love others full out, I can share my happiness without restriction.

Here lies my problem:

The Killer of Growth is Complacency
The Antidote is Stimulation

Which leads to this chapter, "Get Stimulated." I'd grow but then become complacent. I knew the direction I wanted to go, but I was so easily distracted by everything around me. I was distracted by life. I was distracted by what others were doing, distracted by my insecurities, distracted on social media, and reached for more distraction whenever I'd rather procrastinate than face the truth.

I had to elicit change. I realized I allowed myself to be distracted because I wasn't motivated enough. I had to figure out a way to evoke growth even when I lost all motivation.

Take a moment to answer:

How am I motivated?

Well, I am motivated by seeing others accomplish their goals. I am stimulated when I read books. I am reminded of the goals I want to accomplish. Call it stimulation, inspiration or motivation— it really all means the same. *Get Stimulated* means getting to your goal whatever it takes. A type of explicit *positive manipulation*—if you will.

Now I know what makes me happy, how I am motivated, and what is stopping me from attaining happiness. So I started setting safety nets, so to speak. Imagine the bumpers at the bowling alley that prevent your ball from dropping into the gutter. These safety nets prevented me from falling off track.

I'd ask myself, "where am I getting the most distracted in my life?" The answer—social media.

Whenever I knew I needed to be doing something important, I'd reach for my phone instead, and log onto social media.

~

Safety net #1: Implement the Mantra
Who You Surround Yourself With You Become.
Immediately I started to unfollow all the people who pulled me further away from my goals. Anyone I unhealthily compared myself to. Anyone who influenced me negatively. I started following all the people who inspired me. I followed fitness enthusiasts, I followed successful entrepreneurs. I followed people concerned with living a wholesome life. I followed people with similar dreams and mindsets. I turned my social

media accounts into inspiration, stimulation and motivation to achieve my goals. I turned my social media feed into posts that would provoke me to create rather than consume.

I refer to this concept as *positive manipulation.* I know that I have an issue with procrastination. Now that I've set up one of my biggest distractions to inspire me to move towards my goal, I have decreased the time it will take to accomplish it. With this safety net in place, I quieted the noise and narrowed my focus.

If your motivation techniques are similar to mine, I have a list of people I follow in the appendix section of this book. However, if you are discouraged to see others accomplishing goals because you feel behind, you have two options:

1. Change your perception of their success into encouragement.
2. Or tailor this concept of social media to fit your needs. For instance, if it would bring you happiness to help animals, but you feel discouraged seeing others already helping and you don't feel like you could offer more help. Then perhaps instead you follow posts that show all the animals in need. That way you are reminded how vital your immediate aid is.

~

My second biggest distraction is music. *It's my right hand, it's my go to.* Becoming aware of your own thoughts throughout this process is essential. Unfortunately, the truth is, music lyrics influence us, whether we know it or not. So instead of dropping music altogether, I created

Safety net #2: Change The Playlist.

Instead of my typical Hip-Hop, Rap and R&B, I switched to lyric-less music that stimulated my own thoughts. Genres included: EDM—which usually pumped me up, Classical—which sparked ideas, and Nature Noises—which calmed me.

~

My third biggest distraction is mindless activities. Not that they're bad, but there are a time and place for them. When I'm blatantly off track and procrastinating, I've learned to avoid conversations pertaining to any drama, non-sense, politics, and anything else that could get me emotionally riled up and distracted.

Safety net #3: Change The Environment

Anytime I found myself amid a mindless environment, I left it. Keep in mind, you can leave this environment while still physically being present. Simply remove your mental involvement. Most often, I'd physically remove myself. But when that is not available. Simply focus within and excuse yourself from the conversation or activity.

~

Now I've started with a clean slate and changed my environment. The next key step was to officially get stimulated. A sure-fire way for me to get stimulated is to read! You're already doing that now, you're awesome, how do you feel?

The more I read, the more ideas I developed. I also found commonalities with the authors and felt less alone on this journey toward love and happiness.

So continue to read, and diversify your genres. I love self-development books but a great fictional novel is great every so often. I've included my favorite book list in the appendix section as well. I'd love to read any books you recommend too!

I also attended personal development seminars, watched videos online and educated myself any way possible. The greatest stimulation tool is *life experience*. I implemented and experimented with newfound tools. I increased my self-awareness when I honestly answered if things were working or not. If so, I would repeat that action. If not, I would modify it and try again.

After setting myself up for intentional influence—*positive manipulation*— I realized I needed to maintain the stimulation! I felt overwhelmed because I was unorganized! If my brain was a computer, there wasn't enough RAM to load and run all the programs of my goals effectively. The solution—Get Organized!

First, I established a morning routine. I'd wake up and say three things I'm grateful for, ignore my phone, go workout, come home, juice, then spend ten minutes visualizing my goal for the day. Whatever you decide to do, make it visible and stay committed to it! I advocate movement of your body even if it's a simple 5-minute body stretch.

> *Bodies change minds*
> *Minds change behavior*
> *Behavior change outcomes*
> *--Amy Cuddy*

Second, I set schedules and goals (daily, quarterly and yearly). Remember, you are a business. Go back and read your mission statement—your overall blanket goal. Next, your yearly goals. Then, your quarterly goals. And finally, your daily goals.

Some prefer the old school way with an agenda planner or calendar. For the longest time, I used scrap paper for my daily goals and physically crossed them out one by one! I later found that keeping track on my phone is more effective.

I'm part of the *#iPhoneFam*, so I use *Notes* and mark it as my "Action Journal." I write Monday-Sunday with the date on Monday. Then I list all the things I need to do and add the bubble bullet so I can check it off as I go during the day. This causes me to visually see my progress and what I have left to do. I feel awesome when I check something off. At the end of the day when I see a row of checked bubbles, I get excited inside.

Also, I have this idea not to wait until the weekend to relax and celebrate. Once I accomplish my tasks for the day, I enjoy the remainder of the day as if it's my weekend. I'll watch a movie or go out without any guilt because I finished the tasks for the day. That way I avoid the Wednesday burn out I used to get. Whichever medium you choose, stay consistent!

Lastly, I got organized by documenting my day. This is different than writing down your goals list. Document the thoughts, emotions, ideas or epiphanies you experience along your journey. I documented my progress—which is the book you're now reading. Experiment with different mediums of documentation. I prefer writing in my *Notes* app on my phone, and literally writing in journals, but experiment and find the way you are most committed to.

You don't need to document every day. But weekly—at least—check-in with yourself. See where you're at emotionally, physically, mentally and spiritually. Document any epiphanies or new awareness you've cultivated that week. Perhaps any memories that came up. Or dreams! Not only is it therapeutic as hell, but when you look back and re-read it in the future, it's funny to read your past thoughts. *It's stimulating to say the least.*

~

Of course, I play devil's advocate and see that there is such a thing as, *Productive Distractions*. I realize that it's unhealthy to be constantly stimulated. I have personally felt the exhausting effects to be constantly stimulated. Of course, I want to maximize my time. I'm type A with my goals, remember? So I usually take productive breaks. Lately, I've subscribed to an app called *Babbel* which teaches you different languages. It's a neat app because they designed it to be a game. I also logon to

Pinterest sometimes for interior home design inspiration. I'll watch an inspirational commencement speech now and then— which I'll list my favorites in the appendix, you know the drill.

In short, I'll do anything irrelevant to my original task, but still an investment in myself and fun all the while. Are you getting the picture? Do verbs. -ing Learning to cook, cleaning, working out, sleeping, writing, singing. You got it!

Before we close out this chapter, I urge you to take the:

#GetStimulatedChallenge
7 Challenges You Can Do This Week!

Day 1 — Eliminate All Distractions (influence detox)
Day 2 — Create as much as you consume
Day 3 — Question Everything (it's okay to ask why all day!)
Day 4 — Take a personality test
Day 5 — 5 minutes of Silence
Day 6 — No Music for the entire day
Day 7 — Create your 5-year dream board

What's one week of your life? Aren't you worth it? Your future Self thanks you!

~

To wrap up—on *Positive Manipulation*—I've followed these tips to date and increased my productivity towards my goals in a significantly shorter period of time. What's the intent behind intentionally manipulating yourself? For you to be better, nothing more. Literally, for your best interest. For the well-being of you. To perpetuate love, preventative health, mental wellness and spiritual liberation.

~

Take a moment to check-in. Who is it that you embrace? Are there any new realizations? How are you feeling? Is this something you've felt before? Perhaps it's your native Self?

PART III

Identify & Change the Pattern

Chapter Five

INSECURITIES

"A ship is always safe at the shore, but that is not what a ship is built for."
—*Albert Einstein*

Before we begin, I just want to acknowledge how far you've come. You are crazy and I love crazy! I can't say, "I can't believe it," because *I can* believe it! I knew you were capable, I knew you were ready, I knew *you knew* it was time. #AboutDamnTime, *right?*

You've read more than halfway through, you've committed yourself to you. It doesn't matter how long it took you to reach halfway. It doesn't matter how many times you stopped. It doesn't matter if you failed when trying these methods. All that matters is where you are right now. You are dedicated. You are courageous. You believe in You. That is not something that goes unnoticed at all! I can feel your vibrations right at this very moment. Where you are, is where I am. When you are this way, we are one. We are connected. We are grounded in our Truest beings. We are enacting our human rights. We are truly alive.

But listen, this is where the real work begins. The other work you've done to get to right now was the fundamentals. The strong base. They are the most important. They are the foundation. Without those, these next chapters are meaningless. The first four chapters are to increase your self-awareness, to practice using your consciousness. These next chapters will shed light on the cycle of patterns that we are unaware of. When we combine consciousness with an understanding of our patterns, we can maximize our ups and minimize our downs. The quicker we confront our fears, the quicker we can overcome then. The quicker we confront our fears, the quicker we can heal—become stronger and inspire others to do the same.

~

These next three chapters reveal the hidden causes of unhappiness. Once you identify which causes affect you, you can choose to keep them, or let them go.

INSECURITIES

~

As I briefly mentioned before, I experienced General Anxiety Disorder, Post Traumatic Stress Disorder, and Social Anxiety. I experienced heavy amounts of bullying throughout high school. My brother advised me to, "simply ignore it and it will go away, there will be something else that happens which people will turn their attention to." Of course, I knew he had good intentions when stating this, but looking back now, I created avoidance tendencies that isolated me. I avoided and ignored all social interactions because it took my focus off survival. I was more relieved to be at school than I was to be at home. Of course, no one knew because I suffered in silence.

I learned a very important lesson.

> When you don't deal with something,
> it doesn't go away,
> it continues to come back,
> with heavier dismay.
>
> It's as if when you ignore the monster,
> it multiplies in size behind the door,,
> when you're ready to open the door,
> it's ten times the size it was before.
>
> You're still the same size,
> if anything you're smaller than before.
> Because you're broken
> and exhausted from the war.
>
> I'll try to stop rhyming,
> but hopefully you see the theme.

It's a difficult road to recovery from the mean.

I call this *prolonging the inevitable*. We think we are safer when we ignore and deny our emotions. But to ignore and deny our emotions is to ignore and deny that which makes us human. That which separates us from all living creatures.

Alternatively, I've learned, it's more efficient to prepare for the evitable. The evitable is your emotions. They aren't going anywhere. They've been with us since the day we were created. Emotion's purpose is for survival.

Emotions are indicators when the environment around us is not conducive to our well-being. Imagine that our emotions are a safety alarm that rings when our health is in jeopardy. Emotions create energy, to protect us at any cost.

Emotions are a tool. Once you realize emotions are a tool, you can use your emotions for what they are, rather than let them use you. Aren't you tired of your uncontrolled emotions getting you into trouble? Have you ever said anything to someone in a burst of anger or hurt? Have your uncontrolled emotions sabotaged your relationships? Have they sabotaged your financial well-being? Your physical well-being? Your spiritual well-being?

When you commit now—to recognizing the patterns of your emotions—you can begin to allow your emotions to flow simply as they are. They are the *opinions* of your brain to a current situation. You can choose to let go of the *opinions* as quickly as they come up.

Emotions are *optional* for us to respond to, they are merely a *suggestion* of what is survival. We are modern humans, in the modern era. The means of survival in this day mean successful relationships, prosperity and happiness.

When we ignore our emotions, ignore the situation that brought them out, they simply fester and multiply deep within us. Life has a funny way of telling you what to pay attention to. I've found that when we ignore the signs, the signs keep coming back, with more intensity until we finally do something about it. The more you practice mastering your emotions, the more it becomes second nature to do so. Observing your emotions becomes effortless. Happiness derives from simplicity.

Emotions are what you need, become well acquainted, they aren't going anywhere. They will keep popping up until you learn to conquer them. Until you learn to use your emotions and not let them use you—until you see your emotions as a tool, until you are unafraid to immerse yourself in them—you will know bliss, happiness, love, freedom. So, if you're tired. If you're at your wit's end. If you're ready to take charge of your emotions. Let's do something about it together.

~

Use the following guide to model different emotions. The hardest emotions to tackle are those that create insecurities, so we will use those as our example.

In my experience, the cause of insecurities derive from two scenarios:

The opinions others have *over* us
And/Or
The opinions we have *over* ourselves.

Qualities needed throughout this journey: discernment, judgment and honesty. Let's address the former cause of insecurities. *The opinions others have over us.* I observed that our insecurities derive from the conflict between who we think we ought to be and who we are. I've found a simple method to grab a piece of paper, write a line down the middle, on the left write, "Who I think I should be." Think of as many notions, ideas, opinions or judgments others have directly or indirectly made to you. Who do you feel pressured to be? What do you feel pressure to do?

On the right side of your paper, write, "Who I am." Make a list of who you are, for real, without anyone looking at you, and no external motivators like (ego, status, money, drugs, sex etc.) If you have no idea then congratulations—no seriously—because if you truly don't know who you are, you're at the bottom. And there is only going up from here! Your back has hit the wall—so to speak—your road to awareness and fulfillment lie in front of you.

In my case, I thought I should be a college student, a doctor, have many friends, make lots of money, accomplish great successes, to name a few. No wonder why I had so many insecurities when dropping out of college, failing to become a doctor, not having many friends, hating money, and filled with confusion about what success even was.

Then, I listed who I am: I am creative, I am artistic, I love to write, I love animals, I love to create, I love *love*. I can focus on a few quality relationships at a single time. I dislike money because of my childhood upbringing. I love being healthy. I love helping others—to name a few.

No wonder why I'm so happy now, not focusing on the opinions of what others think I should be. No wonder I'm so happy only focusing on who I am. I found myself apologizing or undermining myself whenever I told someone I dropped out or believed in the alternative methods of education. It's as if I *knew* their disapproval and put myself down *before* they could get to me. I hated it. From now on, I repeat to myself when I'm acting as Me, **"I won't apologize for the path I've allowed myself to take, I won't apologize for the path I've decided to take."**

~

Great so we've addressed the first cause of our insecurities, the conflict between who I *am*, and who I think I *should* be. When you realize this conflict, you observe and make sense of why you're full of doubt. You're full of doubt because who you are doesn't equal who others think you ought to be. You now change a simple word: the opinions of what others have *over* us, to the opinions others have *of* us. Now, you eliminate the power over you, and simply observe an opinion for what it is.

Since you observe a comment as merely an opinion, you can choose to reject or accept it. *Opinions are optional.* The ball is in our court so to speak. When we don't feel attacked, we eliminate the need to defend. We can play offensively in communication within the relationships in our lives. We can choose to disempower the opinions others have of us. We can disengage in an argument. All this helps us to live proactively rather than reactively.

~

Now, let's address the later cause of insecurities, the opinions we have *over* ourselves. There are two surefire ways I've combated every insecurity, every fear and every emotion successfully in my life. Here is the first method, it has two parts:

I. Love Thy Self

II. Unearth Thy Truth

When you do these two things, you take power away from the insecurity. Remember, emotions carry energy. We have blockages in our body, that harness unresolved emotions. These blockages take energy away from productive things—things that bring us love, happiness, growth and healing.

When you redirect this energy, you allow room for insights into your true Self. The power of the insecurity over you vanishes. You begin to see the insecurity as what it is, *an* insecurity. It is no longer *my* insecurity, it simply is *an* insecurity. Again, you change a simple word from the opinions we have *over* ourselves, to the opinion we have *of* ourselves. Remember, opinions are optional.

When you do these two things, you begin to identify your cycles and patterns quickly. When you identify your cycles and patterns, you learn what to do to maximize your ups and minimize your downs.

I. LOVE THY SELF

How do you accomplish such a task? First, decide what is unconditional love? In my book, unconditional love is love without conditions. It does not love to expect something in return. Love doesn't love with any ulterior motives. Love is pure, love is light. Love is invigorating, energizing and expansive. Love is patient, kind and honorable. If I am to love myself, I must be kind to me. I must love myself despite my mistakes, despite my cycles of emotions. I must love myself unconditionally without any expectation in return.

I know I am loving myself when I feel energetic. When I feel safe and comfortable. I know I am loving myself when I feel encouraged and empowered.

You may think you see a not-so-pretty side of yourself when you experience emotions such as anger, pity, hatred, anguish, envy, and cruelty. Realize, that this needs a loving capacity to heal from these. Do not shame yourself for experiencing it. Embrace it, it is you. It is all of us. It is okay to feel this way. It's not okay, however, not to do anything about it.

II. UNEARTH THY TRUTH

They say the truth is ugly for a reason. But don't let that deter you from addressing it. They also say the truth will set you free. To which I firmly believe in my life and the lives of others around me.

Emotions are indicators. It means one of two things: your perception of a situation is off, or the situation itself is off. When you consider both possibilities you can track the culprit of each one. I've found that you know which one is the truth because it hurts more when you say it. It hurts more when you read it. It hurts more when you realize the truth has been there all along.

But you know what? It hurts less when you love yourself despite the outcome. It hurts less when you identify the truth and now can do something about it. It hurts less when you take power over the emotion versus it taking power over you. It hurts less when you stop hurting others. It hurts less when you stop hurting yourself. It hurts less when you heal. When you grow. When you become happy in the end.

~

If the previous method doesn't work well for you—fear not—I have one more to share. Sometimes the first doesn't work for me either. Remember you will develop an instinct to know what you need at the very moment. Be ready and willing to adapt.

So here is the second method to overcome insecurities, emotions and fears. It has five parts:

I. Embrace Thy Insecurity
II. Name Thy Insecurity
III. Reverse Thy Ratio
IV. Declare Thy Truth
V. Psych Thyself Up

I. EMBRACE THY INSECURITY

Let them in, immerse yourself in it. Create a safe space for them to come out. Write them down. Share it with someone trustworthy. If there isn't anyone then draw it out. Sleep it off. Learn the Liberating Power of Unconditional Love. Do not invalidate your emotions. Embrace them. Experience the series of follow-up emotions that come along. If you feel helpless, lost and afraid; perhaps you also feel worthless.

Allow for the *pity party* to begin—as I refer to it. Stay with this as long as you need it. Be patient and kind to yourself. If you're wary of knowing when enough is enough, perhaps you set yourself a time limit. I would say, "Okay Toni, for the next hour, allow yourself to mope." When the hour was up, I'd let it go and move to step two.

II. NAME THY INSECURITY

I feel _____. Fill it in, until you get to a concise word that describes the emotion. I feel *rejected*. Rejection encompasses feelings of disapproval, un-acceptance, unworthiness, hopelessness and despair. What makes you feel this way? Is it something somebody said? Was it just a trigger that derives from something in your childhood? Once you name the insecurity you can move to step 3.

III. REVERSE THY RATIO

I feel *rejected*. Okay. When we feel a certain way, we can build an entire list of times when we've been *rejected* in the past. The ratio could begin at 1:1 and quickly move to 21:0. In our minds, we only see the times we've been *rejected* and ignore the many more times we've been accepted. Once you know what you're feeling, think of the opposite.

For simplicity, let's stay with rejection. What's the opposite? *Acceptance.* When have you experienced acceptance? Perhaps, it's when you met a new friend? Perhaps, it's when you applied to that job you wanted and got it? Perhaps, it's when you enrolled in that art class you were interested in? Perhaps, it's when you got into that school you applied for? Perhaps, it's when you got the tickets and attended the concert you wanted to go to? Perhaps, it's when you sent a friend request and it got accepted? Perhaps, it's when you started to love yourself, accept your emotions, and accept all aspects of you? Perhaps, it's when you did things that you wanted to do? Perhaps, it's when you decided to have fun? Turn your perceived L (loss) into a confident W (win). Move to step four.

IV. DECLARE THY TRUTH

What is the truth? Is it conducive to my standards and beliefs? If it's not, repeat how you feel, what is false, and reaffirm who you are. For example, state what you feel.

"I felt _____. Okay." I felt *rejected*. Okay

Don't deny the emotion, and forget it. Remember the emotion and choose to keep going. Second, state what is false.

"I don't _____ myself. Okay." I don't *reject* myself. Okay Lastly, reaffirm who are you.

"I _____ (opposite of emotion) myself. I _____ others."
I *accept* myself. I *accept* others.

Move to step five.

V. PSYCH THYSELF UP

Get *Lit* within. Get back out there. You have successfully experienced, identified, and declared the truth about an insecurity. You should celebrate. Celebrate first by silencing your self-condemnation. Silence your negative self-talk, and replace it with self-love. I'd say to myself, "Who cares that you had an insecurity. Who cares that it took time to overcome it. Who cares that you had a *pity party*. The pity party is over now, Toni. There are a billion opportunities for positivity now. Don't allow that 1 second of vulnerability to scare you away from the world of possibility. Embrace thy vulnerability. Once you do, you strip the power away it has over you. You are no longer a prisoner to its sickness. You're worth it. I love you."

~

I feel insecure all the time. I've found that rather than hiding it or distracting myself from it, I embrace it. I wear it on my sleeve—so to speak.

My husband asked me, "Aren't you afraid to expose your vulnerabilities? Doesn't it make you look weak? Doesn't it make you an easy target for the wolves?" And to him, I replied, "No, it actually makes me stronger, because I am aware of myself. **My vulnerabilities humble me. My vulnerabilities empower me.** I grow conscious of my emotions. Now I use them to my advantage to fuel me in my life for positivity and prosperity. It's not easy to conquer my emotions, but it is utterly worth it."

I'm not saying it'll be easy. I'm not saying there won't be pain. What I am saying is that when you love yourself along the way, when you encourage yourself, when you become conscious, when you forgive yourself, you are no longer a prisoner to your emotions. They are apart of you, but **they do not define you.** They most certainly do not control you. You are in control. You listen to what your emotions are telling you and act upon them with awareness, love, dignity and respect.

The goal is to secure yourself. Secure yourself by committing to love first. Secure yourself by embracing thy insecurity. Secure yourself by identifying it, disempowering it, unearthing the truth of why it's even there and what it is telling you. Is it your perception of a situation or the situation itself? What must you do to resolve the situation? Change your perception, or eliminate the situation. What can you do in the future to ensure your well-being?

Moving forward, I've found that your success to happiness all depends on how well you can set boundaries and follow them. It requires discipline and awareness of your needs. But first, you must experience what happens when a boundary gets crossed. Insecurities occur. In the coming chapters, we will discuss how to set boundaries, and how to follow them.

Chapter Six

THE LIES WE TELL OURSELVES

*What gets us into trouble is not what we don't know.
It's what we know for sure,
that just ain't so.*
—Mark Twain

Humans are cyclical beings. Humans are habitual and follow distinct patterns. If we live in a state of unhappiness, our patterns are usually the cause. We must first identify that which we unconsciously say to ourselves. From there, we can choose to enact change. Often, the change is simply—to live in Truth.

~

There is no easy way to write this chapter. This is our most delicate topic to discuss. It is a topic however, we must discuss. So I write it from the heart, I write it in the name of love, I write it in the name of truth, I write it from a compassionate point of view. Perhaps then, we can unravel the truths together.

There is a list of lies I've told myself, a list of lies I've heard others tell themselves. The lists derive from our childhood environment, our experiences in life and our reactions to life. The list was created as a guide to protect ourselves from pain.

Unfortunately, in the midst to protect us from pain, the list caused dormancy. Lies prevent us from reaching our True Self. Your True Self possesses specific qualities you can only experience while living in Truth. Have you experienced fleeting moments of happiness? Are you searching for sustained happiness? Happiness is a trait only available to your True Self. Imagine that negativity is level 1 and happiness is level 10. If you're on level 1 you may feel level 10 but you cannot sustain it yourself. Like Kendrick Lamar says, "Are you on 10 yet? I live on 10, but are you on 10 yet?"

~

The great news is that once you read the list—nce you add to the list of your own—you become aware of it. Once you become aware of it, you can choose to forgive and heal. Once you forgive and heal, you can free yourself from it. You will no longer be a prisoner to the list.

I urge you to go through this list with curiosity rather than condemnation. Which lies have you used? Are there ones not listed that you can add?

Look, you're not wrong for participating in these lies. You're not stupid. You're not less than. You are imperfect. Imperfection is true beauty. You are beautiful. Be Kind. Be Loving. Soon you'll be able to read this list and laugh.

Lies = Excuses

Excuses are not conducive to a path toward growth. Excuses breed inaction. Excuses breed complacency.

Lies for Denial, Distraction and Avoidance

1. *I Know* — In general, I've said this whenever someone pointed out a truth. Admittedly, I shot this statement back quicker than the other person could finish their sentence. I realized that when I said this, I took away the possibility of growth. Imagine that *I know* was a door. As soon as you say it, you close the door to the *truth*. Your mind will not allow the dialogue to continue any further. You aren't in a state of curiosity or consideration. You are in the state of defense. *I know*, is a tool of denial. One day, I said to myself, "If you *know* Toni, why do you keep doing it? Why are you in the same spot every time? Do you truly know?" And even now, I repeat this quote from Socrates, in times of relapse, "One thing *I know*, is that *I know* nothing."
2. *Adult-ing is Overwhelming* — Initially, everything unknown to us is overwhelming. Once you realize it can be,

you can no longer blame the thing itself for the reason you're not efficient in it. Get yourself together! Literally, get organized, if you're overwhelmed it's because you're unorganized. *Ouch*, right? Schedule your days and times for your priorities. If you have no idea what your priorities are, perhaps that's where the sense of overwhelm is coming from.

3. *It's Human Nature* — It's human nature to be curious. It's human nature to be observant. It's human nature to think critically. These are all the qualities that were created for our survival—to assess situations. I don't believe we were supposed to use these qualities for judgment against one another. Against ourselves.

4. *I Don't Have Time* —- Do you have time to Netflix and Chill? Do you have time to scroll through social media? Do you have time while driving to listen to things that promote your well-being rather than jeopardize it? Do you have time on the weekends? Do you have time during the holidays? Perhaps you're not using your time effectively. Perhaps it's because your goal is unclear. I don't care how busy you think you are, everyone has time. People have said, "Make Time." Then the next word that comes to mind is, "sacrifice." I think this is where we go wrong, it's more of a "trade-off." A trade-off for something you want more. The trade-offs can be temporary. If they are permanent, they simply turn into, "surrender." Surrender to who you truly are, not who you've been. *If you're reading this book, I sincerely think you're on the right path. You're growing*

closer to your native thoughts and your native perspective. All in due time, with dedication to your Self and resourcefulness, you will arrive quickly.

5. *This is Hell, Life is Hell*—Life can be hell on earth, just as easily as life can be heaven on earth. The key is perspective. *The exemption is if your basic needs are in jeopardy.* More often than not, you can change your environment. More often than not, we are afraid to do so. Your life is worth happiness and prosperity. You deserve to live a life that is heaven on earth.

Lies for Justification, Comfort and Reassurance

6. *I Did My Best*—Did you try your best by doing the same approach you always do? Did you diversify your tactic? Did you search for a new tactic? Are you trying to reach success using the methods that always fail? The truth is, you're smart. You're capable of success in every aspect of your life. But you're also so comfortable it's detrimental. When we do fail, we reassure ourselves. We coax our ego to comfort. Change is not curated in an environment of comfort.

7. *I Don't Want To*—Yes you do or you wouldn't be talking about it.

8. *I Don't Care*—This directly translates to, "I'm too afraid to try." Good news, even though you're afraid, you can still try. Even though you have no idea where to begin, you can still try. Even if you've never done it before, you can still try. All you have to do is start.

9. *It's Not Me*—This one is pretty ironic. Your True Self is actually saying, "the person you're acting like right at this moment is not you." Instead, we hear, "the person I'm surrendering to be is not me." Confusing right? In other words, if your True Self is creative, but you paint and hate it, you might say, "this isn't me," but what you're really saying is, "I haven't been *really* me in so long it seems as if this isn't me. In reality, this is my True Self." When you're vulnerable and okay with it, that's the True You. The problem is, we have so many insecurities and fears that come with accepting our vulnerability first. We close the door to opportunity before we even get to our True Self. If you ever say, "It's not me," repeat, "it is me."

10. *The Best is Yet To Come*—I hear and read this one very often. Rather than the ones saying it, living great lives every day, every year, it's as if they are expecting life to simply deliver *the best* without changing a thing. It's as if this cliche comforts us for living another year of life that we don't fully enjoy. The truth is, if you want to live the life of the 1% of population, you have to stop doing what the 99% are. The best takes focus, courage and discipline. The best is right here, right now. But you have to earn it. It's not going to fall into your lap. Stop waiting for life to happen to you, go make it happen for you.

11. *What You Want Vs. What You Really Want*— Have you ever wanted something, but when you got it, it's not what you wanted? Perhaps it's a puppy, and then you realize how much work it really takes. Perhaps it's a new phone, and

then you realize how much it really costs. Perhaps it's a new relationship, and then you realize how much effort and surrender it really takes. Perhaps it's a new challenge, and then you realize how much you're really overwhelmed. The truth is, it's not the item we want, it's what the item will give us. A puppy, a phone, a relationship or a challenge, gives us significance, importance and opportunity for connection. Take money for example. Almost everyone I know says they want more money. What they really want, is what money can do for them. The item—money—is a tool. It's a means to an end. When you determine what you really want that item for, the truth is, you can attain that for less commitment, in less time, for less money—if not free.

12. *I Can't Because They Won't Let Me*—Unless you're a child living at home, no one is, "not letting you." You possess free will. Do what you please. You are in control of your life. A quote from Henry Ford comes to mind, "Whether you think you can or think you can't—you're right." If you believe you can do something, you'll do it. And vice versa. Have you ever searched for something on the internet to prove or disprove something? To support or deny something? Perhaps you've searched *negative effects of drinking water* or *positive effects of sleeping in*. What you type already has a predetermined stance on what you're searching for. The point is, *you find that which you seek*. If your perception is narrowed on what you can't do, you'll find it. If you focus on what you can do, you'll do it.

13. *Traditional Paths Lead To Freedom*—No one really ever defines what the heck freedom even is. The truth is, there isn't a surefire path for everyone. Otherwise, we would all be identical.
14. *I Shouldn't Be Selfish* — I'm certain I learned this one in school. The saying goes, "Sharing is Caring." Of course, all humans naturally care. What no one tells us is *you can be selfish sometimes*. In certain scenarios, you **must** be selfish. In the case of healing, growing and cultivating happiness, you **must** be selfish. It's not an all-or-none phenomenon. The point of being an adult is to make conscious discerning decisions. Of course, no one ever blatantly says that.
15. *It is What It is*—This is the biggest lie that we tell ourselves to justify why something didn't work out. It's our biggest lie that we say to comfort ourselves. If any lie is more toxic to your well-being, it's this one. It's not, *it is what it is.* Do not deny, ignore or neglect room for change or growth. Remember the first one, *I know*? It is what it is, closes the door to Truth. There are alternatives that will mitigate a sense of helplessness. Try a new tool, set a new boundary, follow a new rule. *#Don'tSettle* for anything less. You deserve it. You owe it to yourself, your True Self, to do anything and everything in your power to attain the outcome you desire. If you feel powerless, it's time to learn a new power. Grow. Evolve. Go.

~

Whether we blatantly say these or not, we portray these lies in the actions we take. *Actions speak louder than words.* These lies are holding you back from one of the last obstacles between where you are right now, and where you want to be.

Little white lies become your reality. To know and believe are two separate things entirely. I know it's hard not to lie, especially when it affects us directly—personally. So we ignore, deny and distract ourselves. We think we are doing ourselves a favor when in reality we are simply suppressing that which would set us free.

The by-product of a lie is *guilt*, whether we acknowledge it now, or on our death bed. I found that it was harder to harbor guilt from the lie than the actual lie itself. It's there, the entire time.

Imagine that every lie we told weighed 10 pounds. Imagine that we had just 10 lies at 10 pounds each on our shoulders. No wonder we feel worn out, put out and exhausted.

Imagine if we simply dropped the weight and let it go. How much lighter we would feel? Could our *resting bee faces* turn to *smiles* because we aren't carrying baggage? We aren't carrying anything but ourselves. Like cleaning out the garage when you move, releasing the lies we tell ourselves is liberating! It's relieving.

So we've covered the lies. We covered what the lies do. Are you ready to find out how to overcome them? The mindset and the how will illuminate your truth. *The truth will set you free.* Corny, but true in every sense.

MINDSET

Be Curious, Consider, and Get Out of Your Comfort Zone. Simple. Approach the List with curiosity. Consider the possibility that they may be untrue. If there's even a 0.0001% chance, perhaps it's untrue. Face it head-on. Get out of your comfort zone, because beyond your comfort zone, is where growth begins.

Find a reason to not lie. Find 10 reasons not to lie. Reverse thy ratio in your brain from why I should lie, to why I shouldn't lie. Perhaps, you do it for the next generation.

Imagine a plant. For new leaves to grow tall, old leaves must fall off and sacrifice themselves for the growth of the next generation. For leaves to reach new heights, old leaves must let go. Imagine the lies as the leaves, for the next generation to evolve, we must let go of the lies from here on out.

~

WHEN AND WHY WE LIE

—We lie for self-preservation. To save the ego from humiliation.

—We lie when we complain about our lives. We state a list of complaints, but if we were to write these complaints down, we can see more clearly, whether they are based in fact, or delusion. *I don't have time to _____*. In other words, we lie when we make excuses.

—We lie when we defend ourselves. Usually, when someone points out a habit they disagree with. *You forgot to _____. I know.*

—We lie when we aren't where we want to be. *The best is yet to come.*

—We lie when we are resisting the truth.

~

HOW TO IDENTIFY THE LIE

1. Record—Breakdown Your Beliefs

Write down what they are, think about a way to prove it true, think of a way to prove it false.

I can't do _____ because _____.
I don't have time to _____ because _____.
I don't want to _____ because _____.
I'm tired of _____ because _____.

I can't have _____ because _____.

Think of how each way makes you feel. Could it be reversed? Would others agree? If you weren't the one in question, would you agree?

2. Observe

After utilizing this template in real-life scenarios, you'll begin to notice that your reason for why you can't do something isn't a real reason. Often, once we write down our beliefs, we can see the truth more easily. There are physical and emotional indicators of lies.

<u>Physical Indicators of Lies</u>
-laughing
-heart races
-head drops
-eye contact breaks
-sweat starts
-clamy hands
-close off energy
(fold arms, fidget)
-face turns red

<u>Emotional Indicators of Lies</u>
-defensive in tone and words
-excuses begin
-getting angry
-getting offended

~

HOW TO TELL THE TRUTH

1. Be Disciplined

If someone is discussing your behavior, a great tool when they're speaking is to say aloud or quietly to yourself, "you're right, I am _____." The more we become comfortable considering the possibility of truth, the quicker we can accept the truth.

 * caution: People lie to us. It makes this entire process confusing. People make you believe you are less than you are. That you are not worthy. That you are delusional. People project their fears and incapacities on you. But, once you are comfortable considering and admitting the lies, you will begin to discern true lies from projected lies. Do you remember when I said in the previous chapter that there are opinions others have of us, versus opinions we have of ourselves? The same applies to lies. Some are lies people tell us, and others are lies we tell ourselves. In short, consider the lie regardless. The more you practice considering the lie, the more you nurture your True instinct. You develop an inner awareness and voice to guide you towards the Truth.

2. Be Conscious

In other words, practice. You can't buy consciousness, you must develop it. Through constant surrender of your ego, you can cultivate consciousness. Consider a possibility different than your immediate perspective. Truly, be open-minded, and consciousness will reveal itself. The simplest way to observe your thoughts is to get quiet and get focused. I often meditate on a specific situation I seek clarity on.

First, get quiet. Second, close your eyes. Third, take a big inhale and follow your breath as you exhale. Last, continue to breathe and imagine the situation as an observer. You are not observing through your shoes, you are not observing from the other person involved. You are simply observing, without emotion, as if observing as a stranger. Be curious and consider the vast possibilities of perspective.

~

What we hold in our minds tend to manifest. If you're constantly telling yourself you are in poverty, you'll be there. Despite all the blessings you have, despite all the people around you who love and care for you. If you feel like you've been wronged, if life is unfair, if your job is killing you, you're right. So what's the "fix-all" here? Do something about it. You're worth it. Disprove your self-limiting beliefs. As the famous poet, Kendrick Lamar says, "[The] only limitations you'll ever have, are those that you place upon yo self."

In short, be curious about the internal dialogue you have the next time a situation arises where you catch yourself becoming defensive or complaining. When we pay attention to what we tell ourselves, we notice a pattern of influence. If the current pattern isn't producing the results we desire, we simply change the pattern to produce results wanted.

The hard part is noticing the current pattern. I assure you, with practice, you will successfully identify your current patterns. I assure you, when you come from a place of curiosity rather than condemnation, you will be encouraged to explore the possibilities. You will be empowered to enact change.

The goal of these tools is to support ourselves along the journey to our True Self. If we shame ourselves, we are at risk to hate ourselves. Choose love instead. Celebrate the fact that you even identified a pattern—whether good or bad. You are one step ahead of where you were yesterday. Celebrate the small wins along the way. And remember, the great poet B.I.G. once said, "If you don't know, now you know. You know very well, who you are. Don't let them hold you back, reach for the stars."

Chapter Seven

AND I NEVER TOLD YOU

So I'm telling you now

Now that you've identified some of your patterns, I'm certain you've also identified some of the patterns of others around you. Patterns that may have been projected onto you. Patterns that were full of fear, insecurities, guilt and shame. Perhaps these patterns made you feel that way. Though as you see now, they were not your emotions to carry.

I've heard before about writing letters to people when you're upset, then tearing it up afterward. I tried it a few times. However, there are a few that kept repeating themselves. Common themes and trends I started to recognize. And soon, I started to save a few. I compiled them into a section of my notebook titled, "And I Never Told You."

~

Funny, once you start writing what you would say to the person, it becomes easier to say it aloud. I wrote these a while back, and I didn't plan on ever telling them—hence the chapter title. I was simply going to publish it in this book anonymously and let them read it on their own—if they ever did read it.

While writing this very book, I somehow worked up the nerve to say a few of these things directly to them. To my surprise, they received it well. Of course, I approached the conversation with genuine love and a desire to improve our current relationship. To make our relationship stronger. To establish my needs. As a friend, I didn't want to see them suffer any longer.

The other tactics I tried weren't working, as they were still consumed with suffering. As a friend, I couldn't sit on the sidelines and watch. The only way left was for me to say it head-on.

As I've mentioned, I've lost many friendships in the past when I shared the truth. These relationships were my most dearly beloved. I resisted sharing the truth with them for fear of losing them. I finally decided, I'd rather tell them the truth, even if it meant losing them.

I'm going to share what I've written to them here. The point of this chapter is to show real-life examples of how and what I've said to people I love dearly. This is one of the most difficult tasks but eventually must be done.

Remember, the time it took me to finally speak up is going on almost 12 years. Perhaps you hold off on this chapter until you master the previous ones. You must finesse the quality of love in delicate situations like these. Perhaps you simply read these to see the possibility of maintaining relationships you hold dear. Perhaps you see the strength in ending relationships once and for all.

You can start keeping a list of behaviors and habits that affect you. Most often when I was emotionally charged, I'd write things down. Later, I'd read them over and realize there isn't a need to share because I was overreacting in the heat of the moment. Sometimes I'd delete or trash entire writings about arguments. I'd feel better when I did. Sometimes there were things I couldn't delete because they were reoccurring incidences. The incidences which caused the most pain. Incidences that couldn't be ignored. Their names have been substituted with X for anonymity.

Give it at least a few months before you do this because your perspective might change about a certain scenario. You don't want to say something you don't mean, that's based on emotion, not Truth. Say what is truth, for a fact, proven, recorded.

Once you say it, you shed it. You make more room to be you—like clearing up space on your computer. You spend less time worrying about them and more space to love yourself.

TONI SERRANO

~

OUTLINE OF LETTERS

Dear X,

    (state the facts)

    (how did this affect you?)

    (what does the future look like?)

    And I Never Told You because ……..

    I didn't know how
    I didn't want to lose you
    I was afraid of how you'd react
    I was afraid to hurt you

    What I didn't want
    What I was afraid of

        With Love & Truth,
        (You)

Of course, this is a general outline. I've included slightly varied formats for example.

~

Dear X,

Why do you think you haven't found someone? Perhaps you do not trust yourself, so your mind and heart do not align. Your heart will not open up to allow you to receive that love. Your mind doesn't trust your heart to keep it safe.

Perhaps it's because you're unhappy with yourself, so even when you're putting yourself out there, your sadness is radiating and repelling lovers from your life. Perhaps if you exuded happiness and self-love, more people would vibe and come to you.

Angel and I met when we were playing sports. We were trying something new. We were having fun. We weren't putting ourselves down if we weren't good at it. We kept coming back the next day, trying our best to improve.

Get obsessed with loving yourself, and someone will come. Perhaps you're too focused on the expectations of others to fill such giant shoes—your needs. But you must fill that need on your own. They are to compliment you, not become your dependence.

And I never told you because I wasn't strong enough to. I loved you so much and didn't want to hurt you. I wanted to show you patience, love and compassion. I am so upset to see you so saddened.

With Love & Truth,
Toni

~

Dear X,

The reality is that you bait, blame, project and guilt me.

You bait by calling me with an ulterior motive to fight. You rile me up so you can feel attacked and become victim.

You blame by pointing the finger at everyone else but yourself. You play victim to why things happen in your life. As if they happen for no reason at all, yet share the same cyclical pattern over and over again.

You project by unloading all your negativity and fear upon me, you unload all your guilt, your shame, your envy and your hatred.

You guilt by saying it's all my fault. You say I am the reason for our failed relationship. I am the reason for all of your insecurities.

You've made me feel worthless. You've made me feel ashamed. You've made me feel single-handedly the one to blame. You've made me feel insecure. You've made me feel stupid. You've made me feel that the path I took was wrong, disgraceful, less-than, scum.

For my entire life I believed these things for fact.

It has enabled me from self-love and love in relationships. It has enabled me from my creativity and confidence to live out me, unapologetically. I was riddled with guilt for being who I am. I felt trapped and saddened from within.

I have overcome what you've done. I've told you to your face, many times before. For years now I've told you, and nothing you have done.

I have let go of what happened because I surrendered it.

I know why it was done.

I can no longer be around you for it is unhealthy for me. Everyone has tried to tell you. I have tried to help. Countless times. Books I've read, seminars I've attended, nights I've dedicated to find a way to help. I realized the only way for you to heal is to try for yourself.

In the future I don't see any relationship for us, I do not trust you, I do not think you have my best interest in mind. You scare me, I cannot be myself around you. I cannot hear you lie anymore. I cannot feel your hate anymore, I cannot feel your opinions, judgment and negativity anymore. I surrender.

I deserve love, I deserve happiness, I deserve trust, I deserve support.

I wish you the best.

With love and truth,
Toni

P.S. it's never too late to live your truth. You are capable, you are worth it.

Dear X,

I've been forced to live out my truth and now you're saying you can't live out yours. I hate that what you say isn't what you do. How you raised me isn't the real way you want to be treated. You're a constant contradiction. I hate having to feel guilty because you can't see it. You don't even care to see it. Funny that people love to hear and sing songs about, "surrounded by fakes," but they are all the fake ones themselves—doing fake ass things.

Do—Act—Be, for someone else, but they really are completely opposite. Totally two faced and I can't handle it. Live your truth or I don't f**k with you.

> I try to be sympathetic and understanding
> Patient and Aware
> but the fact that you don't take care of yourself,
> is something I just can't bear.
>
> I wish you knew how much I cared
> to see you lie to yourself day in and day out
> You told me, "how you treat me I'll treat you."
> When in reality, it's "how I treat you, you won't treat me, but you'll expect me to treat you how you think you treat me."

You used to say, "every time you do or don't do what I say, it's like saying f**k you to me."

Lately all I've been hearing is *F**k You.*
You think I'm cold,
you think I'm closed off,
but the truth is I just give up.

I figure, hey what the hell,
they won't listen anyway
So I'll tell them how it is straight up
Because I've tried to be sympathetic,
patient and kind
but clearly they don't respond to that

So maybe I'll be so direct
they cannot confuse what I say
It may come off bitchy,
but it must be said—I have to live my truth.

I felt so guilty for being so blunt
but then I think why the f**k am I apologizing?
Ya'll got everything anyone can ever ask for
You're my elders (as you like to be called and treated)

You should be able to see everything you do.
Take accountability for your relationship and choices.
You set the tone in the relationship.
You set the boundaries of what is acceptable or not.

If you don't respect yourself, I don't respect you.

And I Never Told You

That's my truth for you.

But 99% of the time, instead, I say to myself,
just say you respect them because I feel sorry for you.
That you have no respect for you.

Your confidence must be so low.
Self-awareness so far suppressed.
No wonder you can't see
what is truly best.

I figure I'll just let you believe your lies
I don't want to rain on your parade.

All the things you can argue you have provided
are just as superficial as you try so hard to be.
You may counter that I'm ungrateful.
Which is far from the truth.

My gratitude is what got me through all those years
of patience seeing you live your lies.
Never saying anything about it.
Acting like it was a surprise.

Of where you are today,
like it was a random occurrence
that your life is filled with dismay.

Until I moved out,
and even now, you don't listen,
you hear me
but you're never listening.

You don't respect my opinion
or you're just so completely insecure
you can't muster up the strength
to live your truth.

I've stayed up too many nights,
thinking about your life
and what I can do to help.

And I can try to be pretend
Act like I don't give a f**k
When in reality your life can't leave my thoughts
about just how deep you are stuck

And I sincerely care
I cannot play unaware
And it pains me everyday
I swear

At times I feel like I get through to you
but by the time I see you again
You're even worse than you were before

It could be the money
or it could be not
but all I know is I could be content,
everyday of my life and I wish ya'll could be too.

But until you can, I have to call it quits for now.
And by quits, I mean I'll stay awake.
Sleepless nights to figure out how to get through to you.

I might just take it to my grave,
because you're just too unaware
of how you behave.

And I never told you, because I didn't want to hurt you. I didn't know how to tell you. I was afraid of how you'd react.

With Love & Truth,
Toni

~

That was a pretty heavy chapter, right? I feel that heaviness is what holds us all back from living the life we deserve, living the life full of love, truth and happiness. Once we let go of the heaviness we experience lightness. Lightness is where happiness lives.

You will find upset throughout your journey to You. You will reveal the parts you've consciously or unconsciously suppressed deep within you.

To experience lightness, happiness, healing and growth—you must let those parts go.

You must surrender to your past so that you can enjoy your present. Your future Self thanks you. It will be painful at times. But it is worth it.

The great thing now, is that you don't have to be alone through this journey. There are a million people just like you and me who desperately just want to be happy. Again, it takes effort.

Imagine yourself, carrying 500-pound bricks on your shoulders. Imagine doing this after years and years. What would your posture look like? Where would your gaze be? Probably on the floor. You are literally unable to look up and see the joy in your horizon. You are unable to see the happiness that lie across the valley.

Imagine now, that you've dropped these bricks. What would your shoulders look like? Would there be open sores? Would you be exhausted? Probably.

Imagine what the sun would do to these open wounds? They would probably feel a burning sensation. Imagine what wind would do your wounds? The would probably sting.

When you drop your bricks, you're exposed to the elements. You're exposed to the opinions of people in your life. You're exposed to humility. You're exposed to the healing process.

What I can tell you confidently, is that your wounds will heal. There will be a scar left. What I can confidently remind you, is that the pain is temporary. The pain is not eternal. Conversely, if you continue to carry the bricks, pain is eternal.

Take time to rest, you've survived a war within. Be kind to your body, be gentle to your spirit, be loving all the while. This was the final pattern you must end—the way that others treat you. Now that you've completed this step, you must protect the fruits of your labor. You must set boundaries moving forward.

~

SETTING BOUNDARIES

At this point, you've started to rediscover your authentic voice. The authentic you, not swayed by the influence and opinions of others. You've started to distinguish between your core beliefs and the beliefs conditioned upon you. You've started to identify patterns you follow. You're prepared to discern which patterns contribute to your happiness and which do not.

Now you must protect the path that you've decided to take. You must set boundaries. Make them explicitly known to you and the ones you wish to set them with. If you don't, it's not the other persons fault for continuing to overstep them. Make it clear. Make it known. That way you can't be hurt.

What words, phrases, names, topics, energies make you feel uncomfortable? Write down each part. For example, if you're setting boundaries for yourself. Perhaps you write, "I don't want to put myself down when I make a mistake. Refrain from calling myself names like stupid, worthless, idiot, fool." Or, " I get depressed when I am around negative people. Refrain from or limit time hanging around those types of people."

If you're setting boundaries with your partner, perhaps you write, "I don't like to be called an as*h**e, a b**ch, a d**k, etc. I do not like to be yelled at or said f**k you. I deserve respect." Or, "I do not feel comfortable going out every weekend. I'd like to take turns picking where we go and what we do."

Write down any behavior or habits that hurt you. This is your time to protect you. You deserve to be treated with respect and love. Stand firm in your boundary.

~

Caution:

Of course, be reasonable. Boundaries that contain behaviors such as, "Never forget to take the trash out otherwise I will feel disrespected and leave you," are perhaps unreasonable. Be reasonable. This is where your judgment, awareness and humility come into play.

Remember, it takes time. You will have to adjust and that's okay. You will fail often—as I have too. Remember, you deserve to try again until you get it the way you need it to be. Lead with your heart—with your spirit—for it will guide you.

Chapter Eight

GATEWAY TO SELF

You are now prepared to align your mind and body. To align your mind and heart. You can lead with your conscious heart. When you do so, you allow your spirit to flourish.

Now, it is time to reject, refine or repeat. Go and and re-read part 1. After completing part 3, has your perspective changed? What if you implement these methods for 30 days, then re-read? Have you learned anything new? Anything to consider? Alternative perspectives?

~

Along this journey, you'll rediscover authentic parts of yourself. Perhaps it's spending more time on that hobby you used to. Perhaps it's taking a new class for something you've been longing to learn. Whatever that authentic part is, take care to nurture your Self. Be patient, understanding and curious. In other words, be loving to your Self.

These authentic parts will open new pathways to further develop You. I call it the *Gateway to Self*. Yoga was my gateway, it led me to where I am now. Yoga allowed me to take time for my Self. I dedicated an entire hour to simply breathing and being. I wasn't focused on the past, nor the future. *I am here for the present moment.*

Yoga was merely my gateway to exploring new avenues. Soon, I explored other areas such as massage therapy, Reiki and Eastern traditions. My creativity exploded. I began to write more. I began to love more. And I began to accept myself.

I encouraged myself to heal, grow and be happy. I started to record all the things I did that aided my healing journey. First, I rediscovered my authentic voice. I questioned all of my current beliefs and core values. Then, I repeated what was true. I embraced who I was—a spiritual entrepreneur. I realized that when you own your vocation, you feel like you're on vacation. Time is irrelevant, competition becomes optional, stress turns into eustress, and I enjoy every moment of it.

I proceeded to get stimulated and learn what I didn't know. These wins gave me the courage to acknowledge the patterns that were holding me back. The development of consciousness encouraged me to face my fears and conquer my insecurities. I identified and overcame the patterns that would free me. I stopped lying to myself and started living in Truth. I set boundaries in my relationships. And I kept a record of my progress along the way.

~

All of these tools truly helped me get to a place of sustained happiness. Where I could cultivate happiness despite emotional upset. The quicker you can make *you* happy, the quicker you'll be able to make *others* happy. Whether it be with a relationship, friendship or with your children. You will notice the immediate difference once you learn to identify your patterns and change them for the better. You will begin to notice the reactions of others when you choose to change your pattern.

In my life, oftentimes my husband would be surprised when I changed a specific pattern. For instance, he'd have an accident in the car, then look up at me—dreadfully. Followed by a sudden rush of confusion, he'd ask, "Aren't you going to yell at me?" The first few times you hear something of that nature—admittedly—it will hurt a little. Perhaps you'll feel a little embarrassed—like I did. Perhaps you'll feel strong, for successfully changing a pattern. Perhaps soon, you'll be able to laugh when life happens.

When I changed the patterns that were holding me back, I began to enjoy the moments spent by myself. More importantly, I began to enjoy the moments shared with the ones I love most. This is where sustained happiness lives. When unplanned experiences occur, yet you choose to remain conscious, calm and experience a moment of pause before reacting. You can choose your reaction: a reaction which has proven to bring more unhappiness in the past or choose a new reaction to bring release—which leads to happiness.

~

It's worth mentioning that sustained happiness does have its levels. As you experience more happiness you may soon become addicted to the feeling—a healthy addiction I believe. Happiness is contagious. Happiness is limitless. Anytime you feel less than happy, you quickly begin to learn what to change to produce happiness. These changes become second nature. The more you practice, the easier it is. These changes become effortless.

~

Remember, happiness is the state of ease, where everything flows. You will make mistakes. I make mistakes even now. That is why life is a journey, not a destination. But the good news is, when you make mistakes you can laugh and enjoy every moment along the way.

If it seems like a lot to remember, it's because it is a lot. Remember, this development and awareness of the Self require getting your Ph.D. in You. Isn't it completely worth it? In the Ph.D. of the Self, you get to keep everything you work on. All your energy only contributes toward lifting you up. That is why it's so important to enjoy the process.

And the truth is, I was upset. I was upset about why most parents didn't think ahead, plan or anticipate the consequences of their child listening to their negativity and seeing their regret.

I was upset with most of the teachers who ridiculed us for asking why and challenging the status quo.

I was upset with all the adults who didn't give us *millennials* or *gen z's* any credit; that quizás, we could understand what failure was like. We could empathize with their regrets, their emotions and their conflictions. That we could see a way out—a path to love, forgiveness, and truth. That we could enact our predestined right to chose, to decide, to plan and to prepare for a life worth living—a life worth enjoying for everything that it is and isn't.

I was upset, to be called a *stupid millennial*, but you know what? I'm not upset anymore. This was my obituary to a past self. A self that was shackled to the ideas, precepts and normative's of a society who lacked vision. Who lacked understanding. Who lacked the humility we were forced to face.

I am liberated. I am immovable. I am my most authentic Self. I have let go. I have stepped into my Truest Self.

My wish for you is to unchain yourself from the opinions, judgments, criticism, negativity and abuse, of those who are afraid.

My aspiration for you is to step into your Truest Self. Wear the shoes that fit you—unapologetically. Wear them day in and day out—with confidence, empathy, love, compassion, understanding, consciousness, mindful intent, and bask in the unending, unwavering, omnipotent light, of all that you are.

~

To sum it up. We are not a math equation. We are not a product of our past selves. What we were conditioned to believe doesn't have to be what we continually choose to believe. We do not need to be well-liked by everyone because we are unique and different—in that aspect we are all the same.

When you are your highest self, and I am my highest self, we can honor each other. We are no longer alone. We can live together. Separate, but equal in the decisions we choose to make. What you choose from this moment forward, is your responsibility. You must be accountable.

What you seek will reveal itself to you. Be curious. Be courageous. Be courteous. Above all enjoy the ride!

Sustained happiness is when you can smile internally and shine externally.

All it takes is one generation, one lifetime, one decision, one commitment. Will it start with you? Is it time to start the legacy of love and truth for your family?

In the words of Mary Oliver,

> *"Tell me, what is it you plan to do*
> *with your one, wild and precious life?"*

I've said my peace, what's yours?

Chapter Nine

TONI-ISMS

Along my journey, unbeknownst to me, I wrote down aphorisms, epiphanies, values, perceptions, and poetry. These words didn't quite make the cut into the bulk of the book, but essential nonetheless. Since this book is about the journey to my happiness, I offer the pieces I felt worthy of your time. Here is the list, wishfully chunked into a somewhat orderly fashion.

~

I don't want to go through life; I want to GROW through life.

The Army of Love is Eternal. It Can Always Conquer Anything.

Instead of counting the pages you have left to go, enjoy the page you're on.

Live a life of fulfillment or don't. Either way, laugh and be/do anything you want to do. #WhyNot

I simply wish for people to be healthy
So they can wake up feeling energized,
utilize their body to witness all the beauty in this world,
laugh and love
How can I help more people become healthy?

You are more than just survival instincts. The Higher You is waiting. Connect your Body, to your Mind, So that your Spirit may Flourish.

My mom named me Antonia, I chose Toni.

In a world that's overly scripted, cherish those moments of spontaneity.
#StigmaOfAChildhoodMentality

Don't be possessed by your possessions.

I have so many thoughts on my mind, I feel Best when I let them out.

How you are in high school is how you'll be in life. So practice not giving a f**k what people think, keep your head down and be yourself.

Find the routine that brings out the Best in you, and do it on Purpose, with Intentions to propel your Success to the next level of Growth!

Piece the Puzzles of your Past, to Create a Vision for your Future.

Fruition is the fruit.

If you were to create your life resume, Would You Hire Yourself?

When the thoughts get tough, the thinkers get going.

Think Beyond Yourself. #Perspective

We are all better off Together than apart.

What feeds your soul?

If you never test your limits, you'll never know how far you can go. #TakeALeap

In movies, the camera focuses on the main character. Other people are irrelevant to your focus. Let the expectations and judgments against yourself go, be your Truest self.

I want to be as rich as the amount of neurons in my brain… 100 billion #Science

Stop "waiting" for an opportunity, go CREATE one.
Opportunity is quite literally EVERYWHERE.

You don't need their approval.

Your internal motivation is a muscle, if you don't train it, you'll lose it.

Identity: Life keeps moving forward, you choose to move with it or stay behind.
#evolve

If you don't actively participate in your life, who will?

If you don't voice your thoughts, or write them down, they WILL consume you.

I'd rather worry now, than worry later.

If you THINK healthy and EAT healthy, you'll BE healthy.

Submerse Yourself in the World you Want to Live

Be Authentic: Mind, Body and Spirit

Love Yourself. Love Everything.

Happiness: to Live a life of Abundance, rather than Scarcity

Life is like traffic, you have to give yourself enough time to brake.

They asked me what I was, (ethnicity) So I replied, "Happy."

I'm a task master in the early morning, deep thinker at night.

I am a thirsty ass horse, ready to inhale water, lead the way, I will take the opportunity and say YES!

Seminars are great but they are mostly hype, when you're ready for the real shit, it's the How, it's the Mastermind.

I geek out about obsessing over and living a balanced life because I know at the end it will mean a huge impact on the lives of others.

Be less reactive; more Proactive.

Understanding and Interpreting "Love" to me, is like "Psychoanalysis" to Sigmund Freud. We're obsessed, and deeply compelled to dedicate our lives to it!!!

It takes me on average three years to change and I'm okay with that.

I enjoy self-education a MILLION times more than Traditional.

Don't live for the weekends, live for the time after you get your shit done, on the daily.

We live in a society today where your hobbies can be the source of your income, career and path to freedom. Instead of writing about your hobbies in a college admissions essay, go out and master them!

How can you expect to lift two plates if you can't even lift one.
(Focusing on one goal at a time)

Perpetuate Love not Hate.
Have you ever gotten off the treadmill and had to slow down for other people walking by?
That's how life is, if you let it stop you.
Move around it.

I have an obsessive personality.

I don't have any dope memories when I was young, things I could reminisce on, because my best years are right now, currently living, not looking back, creating massive memories, it's not the time to look back right now. Move forward.

The best investment you'll ever make, is in the youth. Notice there's "You" in youth.

I'm a practical philosopher. You can actually practice my ideas in your daily life.

I listened to so many songs growing up, dissected their lyrics, listened to their words, and now I feel like I can share a story of my own. I am a writer and I have something to share.

Success is having what's important to you. Indicators you might be lying about your success, is when you can't be happy with what you have and when you're still using lower energy emotions daily—such as anger, grief, judgment—negatively affecting others.

You don't have to be good at everything, but be Great at something.

Lately, I've been giving up on people who don't take responsibility, ownership, or accountability for themselves.

Who I am at home, is who I will be around family; around friends; around strangers; etc.

We go through different experiences, but we all experience the same emotions.

Screw Humans; Everyone
Just Needs a Damn Dog
Inaction is a symptom of overthinking.

I guess the big thing is Freedom. We all have it. And we all choose what to do with it. Some people use their freedom to be an asshole. Others use their freedom to be a Kind Human.

Everyone at some point, feels their inner writer. So when it comes; nurture it. Unearth it, immerse yourself in it. It's what will guide you on your next step in life.

~

For Parents:

The sacred vow we make to our children, silently or aloud, the day they are born is,
"I will Love You Unconditionally."

~

Short Passages & Prose

If there's one single piece of advice I could ever give, I'd say, "Be Courageous!" Dare to dream! Try, fail and try again. Get uncomfortable, Face your fears and GROW!

Won't you daydream with me for a moment.
Imagine a world where we don't trade our time for money, to spend that money to connect to other humans.
A world where time is as prevalent as the wind.
A place we can nap under the warmth of the sun.
We can all dance, sing and eat with plenty to go around.
Judgments upon others cease, we are free to express our truest self.
Awe I'd love to live in a place like this.
Now back to reality... or possibly my future one day.

Ed•u•ca•tion
~ an enlightening experience ~
Living your life is the best way to become educated. So define what it is to, "live your life."

You can't become enlightened until you let go of everything you're holding onto, what if this was heaven on earth, you're planning to be at peace when you die, why not peace through this one life you have to liv

I love words like read, and right; because they demonstrate "perspective." Some people will read "read" as a present verb, and others will read "read" as a past tense verb. Read "right" as a directional descriptive word, or "right" as defining truth or not.

I almost gave up on the day yesterday. I almost quit and threw in the towel. But my best friend stopped me. He wouldn't let me fester, he wouldn't let me mope, he wouldn't let me quit. And I'm so glad I didn't, because the rest of the day turned out beautiful. Sometimes we let that "bad moment" turn into a day, sometimes a week, and many times, years. The more we work on our inner awareness to catch ourselves, the more we work on intimate relationships to help hold us accountable for ourselves, the faster we can grow to be our Truest self. My Truth is Love, and I believe all of ours is.

If I had to sum up my year of 2017 I'd say: Accomplishment. Not that I have much tangible proof of my progress this year, but emotionally, mentally and physically— I feel amazing. I began this year with a mission to take massive action to learn more about wellness. Some of you may know I've been a certified Personal Trainer for a few years now. But this year I became a Certified Yoga Instructor (now working at LA Fitness and CorePower Yoga) I also started my Certified Massage

Therapy Training and started my clinic hours for it. I'm starting to read more about Ayurvedic Medicine. Most importantly I wanted to become more educated in the field I feel most passionate about. Not only have I started to learn even more, I'm actually at a place now where I can share the knowledge to truly help others. Sometimes you have to go backwards to go forwards! It's never too late to pursue your passion. I know it's scary to venture into the unknown but I personally advocate facing your fears straight on. This next year is the year of YOU! The year to do what you need for yourself, to take massive action of what you want in your life, to venture into the unknown, become a student again and share it with others!

Be Divine
Let yourself be a host to the divine flow,
it has intelligence and knows what others need in the best ways possible.
Be Authentic
still be you, your own personality, let your heart shine.
Be Mindful
read the room, moderate divine flow.

If I like something, I keep doing it. If I don't like it, I never look back. Because I saw my parents do the same thing over and over, and hate it. I never wanted to feel that way. I saw them have so much regret, I never wanted to feel that way. So when I grow tired of something, I move on. I let go, because there's too much pain in trying to cling to something that's already dead. If it does not serve you, let it go.

~

Short Poems/Raps

#TooBusy

Too Busy for negativity
Too Busy for opinions

I'm just trynna hustle
To execute all our dreams uh

My adversity was Love
I despised money
Because no matter how much my parents made
They still fought
and were unhappy

So I chased Love
not money.

Omnipotent

Dignity or Divinity
it really all means the same to me,

When you do one, you become one
When you act out, you aren't just one
And when we spread this message
The Light will have Won

And be it may, we must admit
It takes hard work to commit

To sacrifice our egos
So that our Humility will grow
It's been said
You reap what you sow

And if we sow seeds of respect
There won't be anything to regret

We will see the outcome of this choice
And see the change it can employ

To see the transformation of the Human
From broken and lost to Whole and Found
No words can surmount

Just feel the Joy
Take in the Sun
Let Love Join Us As One

Forget the judgment
Forget the competition

Silence your thoughts
Sit and ground down
The more we cultivate Ourselves
The more we become Round

To display in our actions
More than we can speak
To display in our emotions
More than we can keep

We'll share some there
We will leave some here
There will be enough everywhere

The Youth will find it
The Lost will too
Anytime anyplace
Despite mans attempt
To hide this good Nature

To hide the healing capacities

To cover up how good we could be
To live among the Trees

Is there an answer?

At first I think we need to be self sustaining
But realize it goes beyond that
Because when you leave them to regulate
Shortcuts will arise

This will jeopardize those of Innocence
Or be it, naiveté
That one day intrinsically we will chose
Sophisticatedly

Another option then,
Perhaps to be controlled
Let few to be responsible
for a designated sum
Regulate unethical actions to keep from

But here lies the introduction
Of something called corruption
In too much power for one

Saddened by the curse
To rise above and run
Away from the temptation to take the easy way out
To exploit the people
Because they have no doubts

But then I become bothered by this whole concept
When in reality,
All we need to learn is respect.

Because when you Respect,
you take Accountability
And with this, you develop strong Sensibility

But that's a daydream for now,
Despite how moved we feel
To change the way we think
That somehow this could influence
Our modern day distractions
Our daily interactions

And have the strength to will
Actions that benefit all of us
And stand the test of time
Because these new morals
Will have tenacity
Such durability
That no evil can corrupt
Not even come close

Because Love will always Prevail
And Lead Us to Light
The Light that cannot fail

Part II

The Light

The Light has been dimmed
Lost and forgotten

Intentionally or accidental
We need it to survive
Without it we are not people

We are not animals
We are not of this Earth

We are not of this world
We are completely hurled

Floating off the ground
We lose all direction

We judge so heavily
We move so hastily
We become saddened and feel so empty

But we have distractions
To make us feel better
Because if we forget
We convince ourselves it all gets better

But the thing we cannot see
Is that we simply delay
The cycle which returns
With heavier dismay

And we flow
Around and around we go

Reassuring ourselves this is normalcy
To be so far from the Light
We fade to dormancy

Boundaries

If I don't like it, then I won't
Put myself in the predicament to be uncomfortable
Because how I live, you don't

And they may see me as weak,
They may see me as insecure
But the Truth is I'm just fighting to be
Who I am and More

So I set boundaries
You know I set boundaries
So I can finesse the skill it takes
Analyze all my tedious mistakes

Make sacrifices and ego checks
To get to a higher state
To remind myself that I'm okay
And this is the process that it takes

To be Elevated,
By so many hated
Filled with Love and Euphoria
No wonder why I can't hang with yuh

Cuz you're energy is too low

And I'm sick and tired for making excuses for yuh

When what you seek
Is within your reach
And none of you, practice what you preach

Hypocrite

You're such a fucking hypocrite
You take one step forward and 10 steps back
You ignore me when I talk to you

The Strong are coming
The Strong are near
The Strong don't choose to live in fear

The weak are many
The weak cannot identify their emotions

The weak promote fear
The weak get weaker by the years

Because they promote judgment
And project outwardly
They huddle in masses
cowardly

The weak can become Strong
Of course anyone Can
But some things are choice

And other things you just Do
Because if you only think about how hard it will be
You'll be behind by two

So to the weak
I bid you Tough Love
Because we all know
The Best is near for You

Role Models: Responsible One

Once You realize you've been wronged
You can choose forgiveness and move on

But if you choose to let it fester
you are to blame for all your anger

This isn't an easy path of course,
It requires discipline, love and discourse

Consistent awareness and analyzation
Many times often, isolation

But if you're devoted to the Cause
to rectify yourself, against all odds

then You will Grow and be Successful
those around you will begin to notice
because in your actions it will show
It will spread to those around you

Then one day when you are ready
You'll share your story to the many

You will become the Responsible One
To inspire others to achieve what you've done

And one by one the world will heal
And erase the need of Good Will

Everyone will have everything they need
And although some will want unnatural things

We can stand by to cheer them on
Because we have a knowledge of ground to stand on

We won't feel threatened
We won't feel defeated

We will Respect each other
because that's all we needed

Insecurities

I question myself
because I want more

people all around me ask, "what for?"

Because I know I can be more
And I know what it will take to Soar

1:16 a.m.

If everyone knew that the end
of Delayed Gratification resulted in
a higher sense of Happiness
that would fix a lot

If people Elevated Consciousness
and Selfless Good Deeds without reward
We would all be better off

If the goal was to identify our
Commonalities rather
than highlight our differences We would
be closer Together

If we learned all of this sooner
we wouldn't have to wait before
it's too late

And live with regret
because we realize we just lost
those we should've Respect

But now we're all just dormant
we've given up our dreams

Now we all just scroll online
to boost our self esteems

It's all buried in
The Lies We Tell Ourselves

Light

This good Light
Lingers around us day and night
It aids us most, in times of fright

Although this Light
Is beyond our sight
It penetrates our Hearts
and Guides us to the Right

We know when this Light is in control
Because the feeling within our Soul

To express our Truest Emotions

To feel isolated by none
To feel understood
To feel Redemption
To feel One

It's the most Authentic feeling in the World

Don't Be Sad My Love

Life is challenging
Life can be drab
Life at times can feel just so bad

It can make us anxious
It can make us miserable
It can feel so overwhelming
It can make us feel terrible

At times I feel blinded
Confused and dazed
At time I feel so alone
I'm lost in an empty haze

But life is also Fulfilling
Rewarding beyond measure
Life is so Vibrant
It makes me giggle with Pleasure

It can make me feel Whole
Make me wake with such Purpose

To be here
To be right now
Conquering what has come

To   be   here
To be right now
To learn from what we've done

I see it clear
I feel it strong
I know that we have Won

So what've I've learned
Life is Constant and Ever-Changing

Don't bank on it
It's inevitable
It's unpredictable

Enjoy it and Leave it Be
And at the end of the day baby
It's just You and Me

So let's minimize our downs
And maximize our Ups
Because when I'm with you
I never feel stuck

I promise to be True
I promise to lift you up

I promise to Grow
I promise to Change
Because this Love I see
Can be so Beautiful

When you Trust in Me and I Trust in You
All I can do is Be Free and Let Go

Let's Live this Life Together
Let's Create Memories and More
My Dear Best Friend, I Love You So Much
You're All I could Hope For

#ShoutOuts

I just wanted to give a quick special thanks to all the people who inspired me to live my True self. Most of these people I have never met in person but I was inspired by the actions I saw them take. If you know any of these people personally, share this with them for I am eternally grateful for their inspiration. I was so grateful the only way I knew to show it, was to pass it on.

Thanks to,
My son
My Husband
Ice Cube
J. Cole
Drake
Beyoncé
Oprah Winfrey
Elon Musk
Mark Cuban
Richard Branson
Arnold Schwarzenegger

J.K. Rowling
Naval Adm. William H. McRaven
Rick Rigsby
Gary Vaynerchuk
Tony Robbins
Dean Graziosi
Stephen Cope
Daniel Klein
Judith Orloff
Dale Carnegie
Mrs. Morrison
Ms. Lay
Mr. Mitts
Mr. Chronley
Ms. Shaw
Ms. Nolan
Ms. Frederich
Master Eric
Master Rhee
Troy
Sugar
Miguel

REFERENCES

PROLOGUE

p. i
"Generation Z: Latest Gen Z News, Research, Facts & Strategies | Business Insiderider." *Business Insider*, Business Insider, https://www.businessinsider.com/generation-z.

p. i
"IMac G3." *Wikipedia*, Wikimedia Foundation, 14 Oct. 2019, https://en.wikipedia.org/wiki/IMac_G3.

p. ii
P, Kim. "23 College Dropout Statistics That Will Surprise You." *CreditDonkey*, https://www.creditdonkey.com/college-dropout-statistics.html.

p. iv
"I am me" Arthur M. Sarkissian, Roger Birnbaum, Jonathan Glickman, Jay Stern & Brett Ratner. 1998. *Rush Hour*. United States. Roger Birnbaum Productions

p. v

Ghandi, Mahatma. "Be the change you wish to see in the world." Retrieved from https://www.goodreads.com/quotes/24499-be-the-change-that-you-wish-to-see-in-the

p. v
Confucius. "We have two lives, the second begins when we realize we only have one." Retrieved by https://www.goodreads.com/quotes/24499-be-the-change-that-you-wish-to-see-in-the

CHAPTER ONE

p. 9
Socrates. The only thing I know is that I know nothing." Retrieved by https://en.wikipedia.org/wiki/I_know_that_I_know_nothing

CHAPTER TWO

p. 26
Walt Disney Company. "Keep moving forward." Retrieved by https://www.goodreads.com/quotes/8594-around-here-however-we-don-t-look-backwards-for-very-long

References

p. 27
Nike. "Just Do It." Retrieved by https://en.wikipedia.org/wiki/Just_Do_It

p. 27
The Home Depot. "Let's Do This."

p. 29
Unknown. "Make it a great day or not, the choice is yours."

p. 30
Serenity Prayer. "God, grant me the serenity to accept the things I cannot change, Courage to change the things I can, And wisdom to know the difference." Retrieved from https://en.wikipedia.org/wiki/Serenity_Prayer

p. 31
Rachel Grady. "Always put yourselves in others shoes." Retrieved from https://www.goodreads.com/quotes/417071-always-put-yourself-in-others-shoes-if-you-feel-that

p. 39
Unknown. "Who you surround yourself with you become."

p. 42
Unknown. "#makemoves."

p. 43

J. Cole. "Good news is you came a long way, bad news it you went the wrong way." Retrieved by https://genius.com/J-cole-love-yourz-lyrics

p. 43
Seinabo Sey. "You ain't getting any younger." Retrieved by https://genius.com/Seinabo-sey-younger-lyrics

p. 47
Baptiste, Baron. Journey into Power: Sculpt Your Ideal Body, Free Your True Spirit and Transform Your Entire Life. Element, 2002.

p. 48
Unknown. "Every failure is one step closer to success."

p. 49
Theodore Roosevelt. "Comparison is thief of joy." Retrieved by https://ryanbattles.com/post/comparison-is-the-thief-of-joy

p. 52 spilled milk & t robbins
Tony Robbins. "Life doesn't happen to you, it happens for you." Retrieved by https://www.davidmeermanscott.com/blog/life-happens-for-you-not-to-you

p. 53

REFERENCES

don't stress over people in your past. There's a reason they didn't make it to your future."

p. 54

Gary Vaynerchuk. "Trust the process." Retrieved by https://www.awakenthegreatnesswithin.com/46-inspirational-gary-vaynerchuk-quotes-on-success/

p. 55

The Notorious B.I.G. "If you don't know now you know." Retrieved by https://genius.com/The-notorious-big-juicy-lyrics

CHAPTER THREE

p. 63

Benjamin Franklin. "Drive thy business or it will drive thee." Retrieved by https://www.goodreads.com/quotes/222189-drive-thy-business-or-it-will-drive-thee

p. 64

Sir Richard Branson. "Being an entrepreneur simply means being someone who wants to make a difference in the other people's lives." Retrieved by https://www.linkedin.com/pulse/what-spiritual-entrepreneur-damien-wills

p. 64

Damien Wills. "Spiritual entrepreneurs only create products or services that benefit and inspire humanity." Retrieved by https://www.linkedin.com/pulse/what-spiritual-entrepreneur-damien-wills

p. 65

Warren Buffet. "The most important investment you can make is in yourself." Retrieved by https://www.goodreads.com/quotes/5205902-the-most-important-investment-you-can-make-is-in-yourself

p. 71

Thomas Jefferson. "If you want something you've never had You must be willing to do something you've never done." Retrieved by https://www.goodreads.com/quotes/1361034-if-you-want-something-you-ve-never-had-you-must-be

REFERENCES

CHAPTER FOUR

p. 75
C.S. Lewis. "You can't go back and change the beginning but you can start where you are and change the ending." Retrieved by https://www.goodreads.com/quotes/9123226-you-can-t-go-back-and-change-the-beginning-but-you

p. 79
Drake. "You're my right hand, you're my go to." Retrieved by https://genius.com/Drake-right-hand-lyrics

p. 81
Amy Cuddy. "Bodies change minds. Minds change behavior. Behavior change outcomes." Retrieved by https://www.youtube.com/watch?v=Ks-_Mh1QhMc

CHAPTER FIVE

p. 87
Albert Einstein. "A ship is always safe at the shore, but that is not what a ship is built for." Retrieved by https://nicholasboothman.com/be-brave-take-risks-2-16/

CHAPTER SIX

p. 103

Mark Twain "What gets us into trouble is not what we don't know. It's what we know for sure, that just ain't so." Retrieved by https://www.goodreads.com/quotes/738123-what-gets-us-into-trouble-is-not-what-we-don-t

p. 104

Kendrick Lamar. "I live on 10 but are you on 10 yet." Retrieved by https://genius.com/Schoolboy-q-2-chainz-and-saudi-x-lyrics

p. 110

Henry Ford. "Whether If you think you can, or you think you can't—you're right." Retrieved by https://www.goodreads.com/quotes/978-whether-you-think-you-can-or-you-think-you-can-t--you-re

p. 118

Kendrick Lamar. "Only limitations you'll ever have are those that you place upon you'self." Retrieved by https://genius.com/Kendrick-lamar-poe-mans-dreams-his-vice-lyrics

APPENDIX

List of Accounts I follow on Instagram for Inspiration, Motivation and Stimulation:
@garyvee
@tombilyeu
@bestyoga
@investorsthink
@mcuban
@thinkgrowprosper
@richardbranson
@tonyrobbins
@thegoodquote
@mental.aspect

List of Books I've read for Inspiration, Motivation and Stimulation:
The Four Agreements by Don Miguel Ruiz
Eastern Body Western Mind by Anodea Judith
The Great Work of Your Life by Stephen Cope
Journey Into Power by Baron Baptiste

The Seven Spiritual Laws of Success by Deepak Chopra
Republic by Plato
Siddhartha by Herman Hesse
Every Time I Find the Meaning of Life, They Change It by Daniel Klein
Groundwork of the Metaphysic of Morals by Immanuel Kant
Unconscious Branding by Douglas Van Praet
How to Win Friends & Influence People by Dale Carnegie
The Creature From Jekyll Island by G. Edward Griffin
How to Talk So Kids Will Listen & Listen So Kids Will Talk by Adele Faber & Elaine Mazlish
The Empath's Survival Guide by Judith Orloff, MD
1984 by George Orwell
Waiting for the Barbarians by J.M. Coetzee
Catcher in the Rye by J.D. Salinger

~

List of Favorite (Commencement) Speeches:
Youtube
Oprah's Commencement Speech
Steve Jobs Commencement Speech
Rick Rigsby Commencement Speech
Naval Adm. William H. McRaven Commencement Speech
Arnold Schwarzenegger The Speech That Broke the Internet

APPENDIX

~

A story for inspiration:

An old Cherokee is teaching his grandson about life:
"A fight is going on inside me," he said to the boy.
"It is a terrible fight and it is between two wolves. One is evil–he is anger, envy, sorrow, regret, greed, arrogance, self-pity, guilt, resentment, inferiority, lies, false pride, superiority, and ego."

He continued, "The other is good – he is joy, peace, love, hope, serenity, humility, kindness, benevolence, empathy, generosity, truth, compassion, and faith. The same fight is going on inside you–and inside every other person, too."

The grandson thought about it for a minute and then asked his grandfather: "Which wolf will win?"

The old Cherokee simply replied, "The one you feed."

~

If you want to keep in touch, join the Facebook community *#I'mUpset* or *I Owe Me Life*. If you want to follow social media accounts for
Instagram: @ioweme.life
Twitter: @iOweMe_Life

For speaking engagements email: ioweme.life@gmail.com or visit website ioweme.life

www.ingramcontent.com/pod-product-compliance
Lightning Source LLC
LaVergne TN
LVHW041250080426
835510LV00009B/674